Adobe® Illustrator® CS Idea Kit

Adobe Press
Berkeley, California

Adobe Illustrator CS Idea Kit

Barbara Mulligan and Jerome Holder

Copyright ©2004 by Barbara Mulligan and Jerome Holder

All artwork ©2004 Adobe Systems, Inc.

This Adobe Press book is published by Peachpit Press.
For information on Adobe Press books, contact:

Peachpit Press
1249 Eighth Street
Berkeley, California 94710
510-524-2178 (tel), 510-524-2221 (fax)
http://www.peachpit.com

To report errors, please send a note to errata@peachpit.com
Peachpit Press is a division of Pearson Education
For the latest on Adobe Press books, go to
http://www.adobepress.com
Editors: Judy Walthers von Alten, Kelly Ryer
Production Coordinator: Hilal Sala
Cover Design: Happenstance-Type-O-Rama, Barbara Mulligan, Jerome Holder
Copyeditor: Judy Ziajka
Indexer: FireCrystal Communications

ISBN 0-321-20544-8

9 8 7 6 5 4 3 2 1

Printed and bound in the United States of America

Contents

Acknowledgments

As first-time authors, we thought a layout program with a good spell checker, a bunch of ideas, and a couple of months were all we needed to bang out a fantastic technical novella. Well, we were naïve. So here we are, some months later, thanking those people without whom we could never have completed this book.

Thank you: Kelly Ryer at Peachpit Press for taking a chance on a couple of first-time authors, Chris Yarrow at Adobe for proposing the concept of this book, Judy Walthers von Alten for her editorial advice and unflagging efforts to keep the project on track, Judy Ziajka for kindly pointing out our errors, Hilal Sala at Peachpit Press for her production help, and Mordy Golding and Patrick O'Neill at Adobe for their technical support with the Illustrator CS Beta.

And most of all, thank you to our family and friends who graciously tolerated us during our summer of authoring.

About the Authors

Jerome Holder studied at the Art Center College of Design in Pasadena, California, and worked as a freelance illustrator in the Los Angeles area before moving to Seattle in 1988. There he helped develop products for a national clothing company as an art director, but he missed the hands-on experience creating art. So seven years ago, he took a year off, bought his first computer, and learned to apply his drawing and design skills to the new medium. Since, Jerome has produced art for Adobe Systems, the Disney Corporation, the Seattle Sonics, Time Warner, and Wizards of the Coast—among other local, national, and international companies.

Captivated by all things creative, Barbara Mulligan's career spans graphic design, marketing, illustration, and retail product design. Her love affair with Adobe Illustrator began when, as marketing communications manager for a small clip-art company, she saw how the then-novel concept of vector art could define her creative future. Since, she has created thousands of illustrations in Illustrator that are now part of the creative content of products by Adobe and other well-known software publishers. Her home and studio are in Port Orchard, Washington, where she can be found gardening with her partner John, and Ian, their little boy wonder.

Introduction

Adobe Illustrator CS Idea Kit delivers ideas, techniques, tips, and tricks that will help you create professional projects by unleashing the power of Illustrator CS.

You will learn to combine your ideas with Illustrator's extensive design templates and resource libraries, and you will explore Illustrator CS's new features such as 3D effects and Scribble fill. The many step-by-step projects are designed to teach you Illustrator basics as well as advanced techniques. Everything you need to get started can be found inside the Illustrator CS software and its application folder. If you have Illustrator 9 or 10, don't despair! You can complete many of the projects with these older versions of the software.

Getting started

Adobe Illustrator CS Idea Kit assumes that you have a working knowledge of computer basics, including how to operate the mouse; how to choose basic menu commands and display palettes; and how to navigate to, open, save, and close files.

When Windows and Mac OS commands differ, the text lists the Windows command first, followed by the Mac OS command. For example, **Alt/ Option-click** tells Windows users to press the Alt key and click the mouse button, and Mac OS users to press the Option key and click the mouse button.

Adobe provides a variety of options to help you learn Illustrator, including printed guides, the Help menu, and online help. If you are new to Illustrator or are unsure of an instruction, see "Using the work area" later in this introduction.

Completing the projects

Each project contains stand-alone, step-by-step instructions. You can complete the projects in any sequence—simply select a project and get going! We carefully designed the projects so that you can follow them step by step even without extensive knowledge of Illustrator CS. The more projects you complete, the more you will learn about unleashing the power of Adobe Illustrator CS to create professional designs.

Using the templates

Many of the *Adobe Illustrator CS Idea Kit* projects use files from Illustrator CS's new, professionally designed templates collection. These templates are customizable design layouts that suit a wide range of purposes, both business and personal. When you open a template, its palettes include all of the graphic attributes used to create the file.

To open a template: Choose File > New from Template. In the New from Template dialog box, navigate to Templates > *<template folder name>* > *<file name>* (for example Templates > Web > Banner1.ait); then click New from Template. The template will open as a new file in Illustrator.

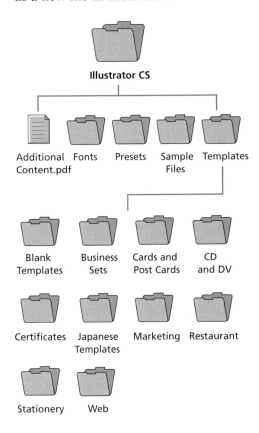

These libraries open as floating palettes in your file (separate from the open file's corresponding default palettes). Selecting an item in a library adds it to the file's corresponding default palette. You can modify a library item that has been placed in the file only by using the file's default palette.

To open a library other than a gradient or pattern library: Choose Window > *<library>* > *<library submenu option>* (for example, Window > Symbol Libraries > 3D Symbols). The library will open as a floating palette in your file.

Using the resource libraries

In addition to the templates collection, you can use Illustrator's new libraries: brush, graphic style, swatch, gradient, pattern, and symbol libraries.

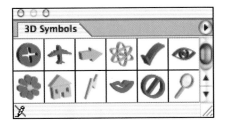

To open a gradient or pattern library: Choose Window > Swatch Libraries > Other Library. In the Select a Library to Open dialog box, navigate to Presets > Gradients or Patterns > *<file name>* (for example, Presets > Gradients > Pastels.ai) and click Open.

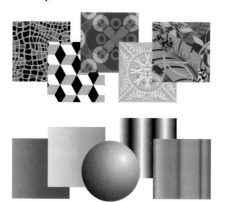

Using the work area

The Adobe Illustrator work area includes the command menus at the top of your screen, the illustration window and a variety of tools and palettes for editing and adding elements. For complete information on the work area, choose Help > Illustrator Help or look in the *Adobe Illustrator CS User Guide*.

Using the tools

The tools in the toolbox can create, select, and manipulate objects in Illustrator. The toolbox usually appears in the upper left corner of the illustration window. If the toolbox does not appear in the window, display it by choosing Window > Tools. To select a tool, click the tool or use its keyboard shortcut; for example, press V to select the Selection tool.

A tool remains selected until you select another tool. A small triangle in the bottom-right corner of a tool indicates additional hidden tools. To view and select hidden tools, click and hold down the mouse button on any tool with a triangle; then drag to the desired tool and release the mouse button. To detach hidden tools from the palette, drag to the arrow at the end of the toolbar and release the mouse button. You can also position the pointer over a tool to display its name and keyboard shortcut.

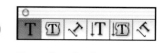

Tear-off Tool palette

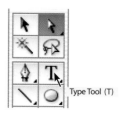

Position the pointer over a tool to view its name and shortcut

Type Tool (T)

Using the palettes

Adobe Illustrator includes various palettes to help you monitor and modify your work. By default, these palettes are stacked together in several groups.

To show or hide a palette, choose Window > *<palette name>*. A check mark appears before the name of a palette that is currently open. To make a palette appear in front of its group, click its tab. To access a palette menu and its options, click the arrow button in the upper right corner of the palette.

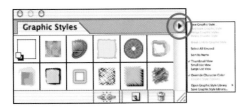

Selecting and deselecting objects

Before you can modify an object or artwork, you must distinguish it from the objects around it. You do that by selecting the object with a selection tool (the Selection, Direct Selection, or Group Selection tool) or command. When you are instructed to select an object and no tool is specified, use the Selection tool. Whenever you need to use the Direct Selection tool (to select individual anchor points or segments on a path) or the Group Selection tool (to select an object within a group), the instructions will direct you to the appropriate tool.

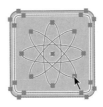

Selection tool

Direct Selection tool

Direct Selection tool (press Alt/Option)

Group Selection tool

To deselect an object, click anywhere on a blank section of the artboard, choose Select > Deselect, or press Ctrl/Command+Shift+A.

Create Marbled Backgrounds

Create impressive illustrations with the Blend tool and the brush and symbol libraries.

■ **C**reating swirling, twirling marble backgrounds is a quick, easy technique to master when you use the liquify tools in Illustrator. In this project, you will learn how to distort an object's shape and path direction. You'll get more practice with the liquify tools—Warp, Pucker, Twirl, Bloat, Scallop, Crystallize, and Wrinkle—as you learn how to create a hairy dog and a free-flowing flower.

1 **Create the basic shapes.** The marble background shown in this example was created using 11 basic shapes.

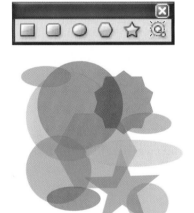

Open a new file. Select a basic shape tool in the toolbox and, on the artboard, drag to create the shape. Repeat using other shape tools until you have as many shapes as you want. For a more complex marble and less white space, use dense overlapping shapes. Select the shapes and recolor them using the Color palette or a swatch library (Window > Swatch Libraries).

To make the shapes partially transparent, select all of the shapes, choose Window > Transparency, and enter a new opacity value (50% in this example).

2 **Select the Twirl tool and adjust the settings.** In the toolbox, click the Warp tool, hold down the mouse button to display the grouped tools, and drag to the right to select the Twirl tool. (Continue dragging right to the tearoff arrow to create a floating palette of the liquify tools.)

Double-click the Twirl tool to adjust its settings. To create a marbled effect, the most important settings are the width, height, intensity, and twirl rate. Set the brush dimensions to about half the size of the image you want to distort. The higher you set the intensity and twirl rate, the faster your image will distort. Try different settings until you find the right combination for your project.

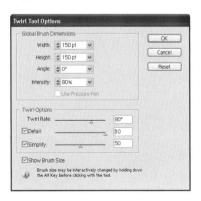

Note: Selecting a liquify tool changes the pointer to a circular brush icon. You can change the brush size in the tool dialog box or as you work. To change the size interactively, hold down Alt/Option and drag until the circular brush icon is the desired size; to keep the icon a circle, hold down Alt/Option+Shift.

3 Twirl the shapes. In case you need to restart from scratch, copy your shapes and paste them to the side of the artboard. Using the Twirl tool changes the image permanently, and its effects cannot be undone (unlike a live effect, which can be removed in the Appearance palette).

Press Ctrl/Command to choose the Selection tool and drag to select all of your basic shapes. Then, with the Twirl tool in the toolbox selected, drag the brush across the shapes using even, fluid, circular motions. This is the fun part, but be patient: sometimes it takes several tries to achieve the desired results.

The faster you drag, the slower the shapes will distort. Stop every now and then to review your progress and then continue twirling. If you hold down the mouse button too long over a particular area, you will create a circular swirl; either select Edit > Undo or use the Twirl brush to push around the edges until the swirl blends back into the other swirling shapes.

Continue sweeping the brush until the shapes appear completely random and organic and blend evenly into each other.

4 **Crop the background with a clipping mask.** Select the marbled background, use the Scale tool in the toolbox to enlarge the image if necessary, and group the individual shapes (Object > Group). The marble you've created may not look great yet, but a few more steps will transform the shape into a beautiful and interesting background.

To create a clipping shape (a rectangle in this example), use the Rectangle tool to draw a rectangle. In the Color palette, set the rectangle's fill and stroke to None. Using the Selection tool, select the background; then Shift-click the clipping shape to add it to the selection. Choose Object > Clipping Mask > Make. Deselect.

Note: The key to a successful clipping mask is to make sure that the mask (in this case, the rectangle) is in front of the object that you want clipped (in this case, the background). To move an object in front, choose Edit > Cut and then Edit > Paste in Front.

5 **Add a background color.** To create a richer look, add a colored shape behind the marbled background. Choose the Direct Selection tool in the toolbox and select the rectangular shape you used for the clipping mask; choose Edit > Copy. Use the Selection tool to select the entire image, background, and clipping mask. Choose Edit > Paste in Back; do not deselect yet. The Paste in Back command pastes your copied shape behind the marbled background. Using the Color palette, choose a color for the new background shape (this example used a green and brown gradient).

6 **Add a few quick effects.** Using the Direct Selection tool, double-click the marbled shape. You want to add the effect only to the marble, not to the clipping mask or to the background shape. Choose Effect > Stylize > Inner Glow. This example uses the default settings; for a hazier effect, increase the blur. Click OK.

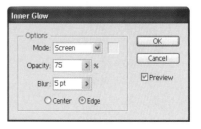

To make the marbled colors electric, with the marbled shapes selected, choose Effect > Blur > Radial Blur. Set the blur amount to 10 and click OK.

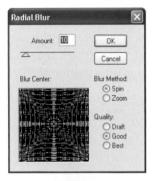

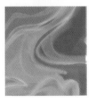

⊙ **Note:** A very large blur amount (20 or higher), will make the shapes unrecognizable—a neat effect in itself!

1 **Create the initial cap letter.** For the maximum amount of marble, choose a thick, bold font. With the Type tool, enter your letter. Click the Direct Selection tool in the toolbox and choose Type > Create Outlines. In the Swatches palette, select the Rainbow gradient.

2 **Copy your original marbled shapes and recolor.** Open a new document and paste into it a copy of the marbled background you created for this project. You will recolor this background using the Color Combinations gradient library.

To recolor the shapes, choose Window > Swatch Libraries > Other Library > Presets > Gradients > Color Combinations.ai, and click Open.

Unfortunately, the gradient libraries are not as easy to access as the other content included in Illustrator CS. Gradients are in the Presets folder, which is in the Illustrator CS folder, located in your operating system's Applications folder.

With the Direct Selection tool, click an individual shape in the marbled background and then select a gradient in the Color Combinations gradient palette. Repeat this step for the remaining shapes to recolor them with coordinating gradients.

3 **Create the clipping mask.** Select the entire letter and copy it. Select the marbled background, drag it on top of the letter, and choose Edit > Paste in Front to paste a copy of the letter at the top of the artwork. In the Color palette, select a fill and stroke of None.

With the letter still selected, click the Selection tool in the toolbox, hold down Shift, and click the background to add it to the selection. With the top letter and the background selected, choose Object > Clipping Mask > Make.

Variation: Create fun design elements with simple twirls

1 **Create a simple twirl.** Using any of the basic shape tools, create three or four simple shapes; color them and then make them partially transparent using the Transparency palette. Select the Twirl tool and Alt/Option+Shift-drag until the circular brush icon is slightly larger than the basic shapes. Click the shapes and hold down the mouse button until the shapes twirl around each other. The longer you hold down the mouse button, the thinner the colored swirls become.

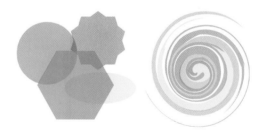

2 **Use the twirl as a design element.** Use the twirl you just created as its own design element or combine it with a simple image. The example here uses the Figure with Heart symbol from the People symbol library.

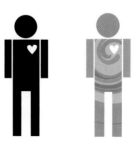

Use the handy tools in the Warp palette to create unique designs. Apply these tips and techniques.

• Start by making a copy of your original image. The tools in the Warp palette permanently change an image, unlike live effects, which can be removed. Alternatively, you can also use the multiple undos available in Illustrator to revert easily to a previous state.

• Remember that a little distortion goes a long way. Both examples shown here were distorted using only 10 to 20 mouse-clicks. For more control, work on individual shapes and distort one shape at a time.

• For the most variation, change the brush (the circular icon that defines the size of the distortion area) many times throughout the process. To change the brush size and tool settings, double-click any tool to display its settings dialog box. To change the brush size interactively, Alt/Option-drag the brush to the desired size, and press Shift to constrain the brush to a circle.

To create the furry dog shown here, open the Ornament brush library (Window > Brush Libraries > Decorative_Ornaments) and drag the dog image onto the artboard. Delete the bounding box around the image. Select the Crystallize tool and click around the shapes, dragging the brush outward to create long strands of fur. For the final details, use the Wrinkle tool to make minor adjustments. To complete the transformation, recolor the dog and fill the mouth shape with a pink and black gradient.

To make this flower, open the Foliage_Flowers library (Window > Brush Libraries > Foliage_Flowers) and drag the Gerbera daisy image onto the artboard. To distort the shape, double-click the Pucker tool in the toolbox, decrease the intensity to 20%, and click randomly on the flower to distort the petals. Use the Bloat tool to make the petal shapes fatter. To complete the transformation, use the Direct Selection tool to select various petals and then choose Effect > Stylize > Drop Shadow.

To distort the center, use the Scallop tool. Set the brush diameter slightly larger than the flower center. Without selecting the shape, center the brush over the shape and click once. That's all there is to it!

Logo
Food
Decorative Elements
symbol libraries

Artistic_Calligraphic
brush library

Geometric 1
pattern library

Image Effects
Buttons and Rollovers
graphic styles libraries

Design the 10-Minute Logo

Logo comps can be made in a snap with a little imagination and the Ilustrator CS symbol libraries.

Making minor changes to existing symbol art is a quick and easy way to create unique, creative logos. This example shows you three simple techniques. You will learn how to customize a symbol using calligraphic brushes, pattern fills, and styles.

1 **Open the symbol library.** Open a new document. Choose Window > Symbol Libraries > Logos. Scroll if the symbol isn't visible. The first example uses the Leaf symbol.

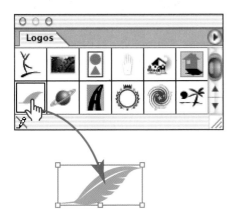

Drag the symbol onto the artboard. The symbol will automatically be added to your document Symbols palette. Close the Logos symbol library to avoid confusing it with your document-specific Symbols palette.

2 **Break the symbol instance.** With the symbol still selected in the Symbols palette, click the Break Link to Symbol button.

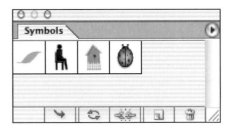

3 **Edit the image using the Appearance palette.** You will change the symbol's stroke and fill. With your image selected, choose Window > Appearance. Because this image is grouped, you must double-click Contents to view its attributes.

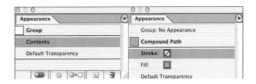

Click Stroke, choose Window > Stroke, and in the Stroke palette, enter 0.5 point as the stroke weight. To color the stroke the same green as the fill, make the Color palette active, and drag the fill over the Stroke box. Select the fill and click None.

4 **Apply the calligraphic brush.** Choose Window > Brush Libraries > Artistic_Calligraphic. Click the arrow button to display the pop-up menu and choose List View. This view makes it easier to see the brush names. With your image selected, click the 1 pt Flat brush. This applies the brush to the selected artwork.

Artistic brushes can add an elegant hand-drawn look. Calligraphic artists spend years honing a technique that you've achieved in only minutes.

Note: Experiment with calligraphic and other artistic brushes by selecting your image and clicking through the Brushes palette until you find the right combination of stroke weight and brush effect. Each time you click a brush, it is added to your document's brush library.

Variation: Add a pattern to enhance simple black-and-white images

1 **Open the symbol library.** Choose Window > Symbol Libraries > Food. This example uses the Chicken symbol. Drag the symbol onto the artboard, and click the Break Link to Symbol button in the Symbols palette to break its link.

2 **Open the pattern library.** Choose Window > Swatch Libraries > Other Library > Presets > Patterns > Decorative > Decorative_Geometric 1 Color and click Open.

3 **Apply the pattern.** Select the Direct Selection tool in the toolbox (the hollow arrow). Hold down Alt/Option and click to select only the body. With the body selected, click the pattern of your choice (here, Hexagon Persian).

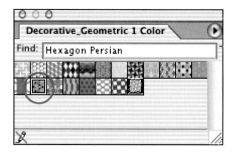

The pattern is automatically added to your document's Pattern palette.

Select the chicken and add a 0.5 pt gray stroke. In the Appearance palette select the fill and choose Window > Transparency, and set the opacity to 80%.

4 **Adjust the pattern.** You can adjust patterns in many ways. To change the way your pattern tiles within the boundary of the image, select the image and hold down the tilde (~) key, and press the keyboard arrow keys until you achieve the desired results. This pattern was adjusted by moving the pattern to the left until a black triangle became the perfect beak.

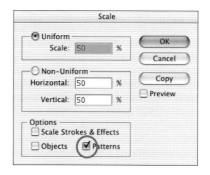

Note: To change the scale of your pattern, select your image and double-click the Scale tool in the toolbox. In the Scale dialog box, select Uniform Scale and enter 50%, and for Options deselect Objects and select Pattern. You can also use any of the transform tools to alter your pattern.

□ **Variation: Use preset styles to add eye-popping dimension to your logo**

1 **Open the symbol library.** Choose Window > Symbol Libraries > Decorative Elements. This example uses the Lilypad symbol.

Drag your image to the desktop and break the symbol instance by clicking the Break to Symbol button at the bottom of the Symbols palette.

2 **Open the style libraries.** This example uses two different styles. Choose Window > Graphic Styles Libraries > Image Effects and then Window > Graphic Styles Libraries > Buttons and Rollovers.

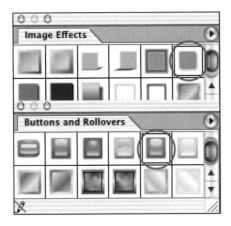

3 **Apply and customize the flower style.** With the Direct Selection tool, select only the flower petals. In the Image Effects palette, click Drop Shadow Soft. With the flower still selected, in the Color palette click the fill and click in the color bar to select a color.

4 **Apply and customize the leaf style.** With the Direct Selection tool, select

the lily pad leaf and all of its pieces; then click the Glass Button Green style in the Buttons and Rollovers graphic styles library.

To remove the floating shadow on the flower, with the leaf still selected choose Window > Appearance. In the palette, select the second white fill in the palette and delete it by clicking the palette's Trash button. To soften the drop shadow, double-click the drop shadow and, in the Drop Shadow dialog box, decrease the X offset, Y offset and the blur.

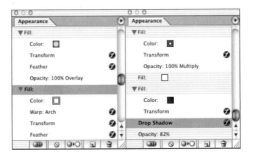

⊙ **Note:** To change the drop shadow on an existing image or style, you must use the Appearance palette. Choosing Effect > Stylize > Drop Shadow will apply a second shadow to your image.

DESIGN TIP: Use a symbol's basic shape as a building block

To customize a symbol, start with its basic shape, and then use Illustrator tools and features to create your new design.

Simplify a symbol by tracing over it with the Pen tool. Add a fill or stroke. Then create a new symbol from the selected illustration by clicking the New Symbol button at the bottom of the Symbols palette. In the palette, double-click the new symbol and name it.

Symbol Libraries > Web Buttons and Bars > Button 37 Normal

Add pizzazz to a symbol with color and simple effects. Create two ellipses and use the Shear tool to add perspective. The Add Arrowhead effect transforms a simple stroke into a graphic flower. Then create a new symbol from your selection.

Symbol Libraries > People > Sitting in Chair

Add your own special touch by breaking the symbol instance and changing the elements. With the Direct Selection tool, you can stretch the house and move the windows. The simple fork-and-spoon fence was created with the Pen tool. When you have finished creating your new illustration, group the new elements with the original symbol, and create a new symbol.

Symbol Libraries > Buildings > House 1

Project 3

Design a Business Card in 15 Minutes

Combine the versatility of a scatter brush with a clipping mask to create an attractive, high-impact business card.

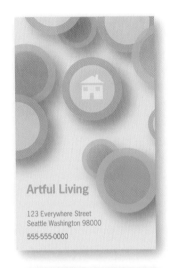

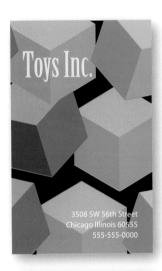

■ **C**reating business cards is a breeze when you use scatter brushes and clipping masks. This project shows you how to get the most impact by increasing the size and spacing of the individual scatter brush elements and then artfully cropping the brush with a clipping mask. You'll also learn some great tips for designing a card with a full bleed.

1 **Get started.** All of these cards were built using the Business Card 2 Blank template. To open the template, choose File > New from Template > Blank Templates > Business Card 2_ Blank.ait and click New from Template. This opens a copy of the original template. Save and name your new document. To open the brush library, choose Window > Brush Libraries > Decorative_Scatter.

◯▶ **Note:** All of these examples use scatter brushes from the Decorative Scatter brush library.

Brush libraries are listed by theme and most contain an assortment of scatter, art, and pattern brushes. To easily tell one type of brush from another, go to the Brushes palette, click the arrow

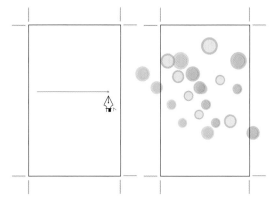

button and choose List View from the palette menu to display the brush icons.

2 **Create the scatter brush.** Scatter brushes are typically applied to a path created by the Paintbrush, Pencil, Pen, or Line Segment tool. Start by drawing a line with no fill and then click the Dots brush in the Brushes library to apply the scatter brush.

You can change the size, spacing, scatter, and rotation of the individual elements that make up a scatter brush. Select your line and double-click the brush in the Brushes palette. Enter your new settings and click Preview to view the changes. Click OK and then click Apply to Strokes.

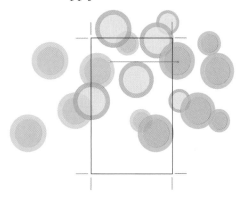

3 **Add the other elements.** Select the Type tool in the toolbox and enter your text. Add extra elements. This example uses the Home symbol from the Web Icons symbol library.

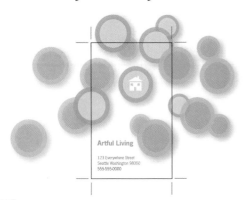

4 **Create the clipping mask.** First you'll draw the shape that will become your mask. Select the Rectangle tool in the toolbox and, using the artboard boundary line as a guide, drag a rectangle shape from the left bottommost point of the template to the top right. Select a fill and stroke of None. Click the Selection tool, hold down Shift, and select the brush stroke and the rectangle you just drew. Choose Object > Clipping Mask > Make. Using the Direct Selection tool, enlarge the mask by dragging each side outward by at least 10 points to provide some extra bleed.

Variation: Use a scatter brush element as a photographic clipping mask

Most scatter brushes are created from an individual art element. Use these little elements as creative clipping masks for simple photographs.

1 **Select your image.** Choose a brush that has a simple shape. This example uses Squares 1 from the Decorative Scatter brush library. Drag the brush element to an open area on the artboard, select the brush element, and choose Object > Ungroup twice.

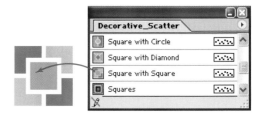

To enlarge the brush element, select it and then double-click the Scale tool and enter a larger value in the dialog box. With the Selection tool, click the part of the element that you want to use as the clipping mask. Set the fill and stroke to None.

2 **Place your photograph.** Because you are working with such a small space, choose a photo that has minimal detail. Choose File > Place and select and place the photo. With the photo still selected, choose Object > Arrange > Send to Back. Center the photo behind the brush element. If desired, resize the photo by selecting it and double-clicking the Scale tool.

Variation: Create a dynamic background by duplicating your brush strokes

1 **Duplicate the brush.** Select your brushed stroke, Alt/Option-drag to create the second stroke, and choose Object > Transform > Transform Again. This will create a third stroke. Double-click the brush (this example uses Decorative Scatter-Cubes) in the Brushes palette and enter a larger size.

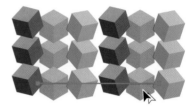

3 **Create the clipping mask.** Click the Selection tool, hold down Shift, and select the photograph and the clipping shape. This example uses the inside square. To clip the photo, choose Object > Clipping Mask > Make. Recolor the outside shapes to match your color scheme.

2 **Create the clipping mask.** Draw a rectangle shape and with the Selection tool, hold down Shift, and select the rectangle clipping shape and the three brush strokes. Choose Object > Clipping Mask > Make. If desired, select the brush strokes using the Direct Selection tool and reposition them within the mask.

FAMILY
ADOPTION
SERVICES

123 EVERYWHERE STREET
SEATTLE WASHINGTON 98000
555-555-0000

Toys Inc.

123 Everywhere Street
Seattle Washington 98000
555-555-0000

Variation: Add styles and effects to make your design unique

1 **Adjust the brush setting.** Draw a small line using the Pen tool and click a scatter brush in the Decorative_ Scatter brush library (this example uses Decorative Scatter_Cross in Circle). With your brushed stroke selected, double-click the brush in the Brushes palette, and increase the spacing so that the circles just start to touch each other.

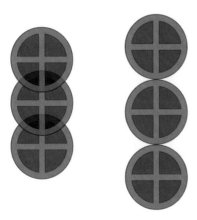

Note: Click Preview in the Scatter Brush Options dialog box to view how different spacing settings will effect your brushed stroke. You may need to click Preview again to refresh the preview each time you enter a different setting. When you have the spacing you like, click OK and then click Apply to Strokes.

2 **Add an effect.** Filters and effects offer a great way to add your own distinctive touches. Select your brush element and choose Effect > Pixelate > Pointillize, and enter a cell size. This example uses the default setting.

Add transparency to the selection to make the effect more subtle. Choose Window > Transparency and, in the palette, enter an opacity value. This technique was also used on the background. Experiment with other Pixelate options to create interesting textures.

With clever design and layout, you can incorporate a full bleed into your professionally printed business card at a fraction of the cost.

Professionally printing a piece with a full bleed (in which the image goes right to the edge of the paper) can be expensive. In the case of business cards, most small- to medium-size print houses run cards four- to eight-up on a larger sheet of paper. Next time you have a business card to design, put that extra space to use by making it part of the adjacent card's design.

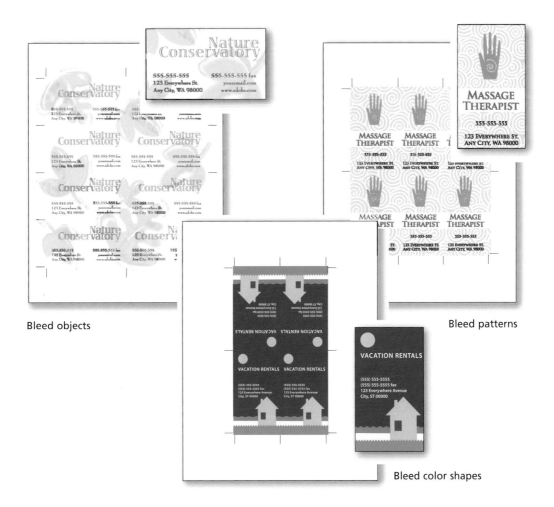

Bleed objects

Bleed patterns

Bleed color shapes

Keep in mind that a very heavy application of ink may result in extra ink or wash-up charges. When you lay out your business cards, be sure not to leave any gutter space between the cards. The cards must be flush with each other.

Materials: █ **Project 4**

*DVD Booklet 1
Outside
Presentation 4
templates*

*Neon graphic
styles library*

Your photos

Design a Brochure in 30 minutes

Make quick work of color scheme, type placement, and cutting-edge techniques with professionally designed templates.

■ **W**hen the amount of text—and the budget—is modest, a mini-brochure is the perfect solution. This project lets you break away from the traditional tri-fold letter design, and revamp an existing DVD Booklet template. The presentation template inspires the new color scheme and includes its own Swatches palette, making the job of recoloring simple and quick. The project also includes great tips for selecting like colors, replacing photographs, and formatting text using the new Illustrator CS Character Styles palette.

1 **Open the template.** Choose File > New from Template > Templates > CD and DVD > DVD 1 Booklet Outside.ait. This command sequence opens a copy of the original template. Save and name your new document.

2 **Open the Swatches palette.** To import the color scheme for your brochure, choose Window > Swatch Libraries > Other Library > Templates > Marketing > Presentation 4 Content.ait. This opens the Swatches palette created inside the presentation template. The template name will appear on the palette tab. Shift-click within the palette to select the swatches you would like to use and drag them into your document-specific Swatches palette.

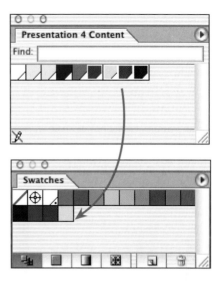

The presentation template is in RGB color mode, but the file in which you're working is CMYK. When transferred to your document Swatches palette, the swatches will convert to CMYK. To avoid confusion, rename your swatches by double-clicking the color swatch and entering the CMYK value or a descriptive name.

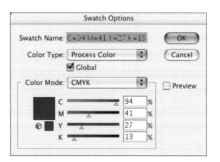

▶ **Note:** To round off the CMYK values, double-click the swatch, press Tab to highlight the individual value boxes, and press the up or down arrow keys on your keyboard. Changing the values by 1% usually won't affect the appearance of your colors, but it will make it much easier for you to use the values to name the swatches.

3 **Change the color scheme.** First, using the Selection tool, delete the unwanted graphics.

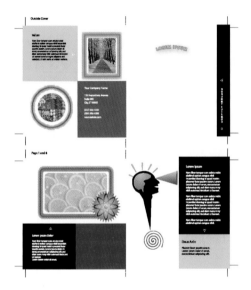

With the Direct Selection tool, select the top-left yellow box. Choose Select > Same > Fill Color. Click the new Blue swatch. Repeat this process for the remaining color boxes, changing all to match your new color scheme.

To change the color of the gradient fill on the brain graphic, select the Direct Selection tool, click the brain shape, and then choose Window > Gradient. Drag the Violet swatch from your Swatches palette over the red gradient slider and drag the Blue swatch over the yellow. Repeat this process with the atom and triangular telescope gradients.

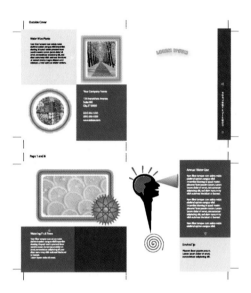

To recolor the headline, select and choose Window > Appearance. You must use this palette to change the headline's attributes because it is a live effect. In the Appearance palette, click Fill and change the fill color to white, then click Stroke and change the stroke color to black. In the Stroke palette, decrease the weight to 1 point.

4 **Customize headlines and replace text.** Start with the vertical type on the right. Select the Type tool and triple-click the text to select it; then type your own text.

To change the headline text, highlight the type with the Type tool and enter your new headline. If you want to adjust the arc, select the type with the Direct Selection tool. In the Appearance palette, double-click Warp:Arc, adjust the percent of horizontal blend, and then click Preview to view the adjustment. Click OK to apply it.

Use the Type tool to select text in the individual type blocks and enter the new text.

5 **Create the neon borders.** Make this your quickest revision by using the Neon Styles library. Choose Window > Graphic Styles Libraries > Neon Effects. Select one of the borders with the Direct Selection tool and click the Thin Aqua Neon style in the Neon Effects palette. Repeat this process for the other borders.

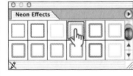

6 **Add a neon symbol.** Choose Window > Symbol Libraries > Weather, and drag the Sun symbol to the artboard. Click the Break Link to Symbol button on the Symbols palette, and with the image still selected, select Thin Yellow Neon in the Neon Effects library.

Note: Neon is a simple effect created by placing consecutively smaller strokes on top of each other. Apply a neon border from the Neon Effects library, open the Appearance palette, and examine the strokes; each started with one stroke that was duplicated multiple times by choosing Duplicate Item from the Appearance palette menu. To change the color of a neon style, click the individual stroke attributes in the Appearance palette and recolor. The glow is three transparent strokes with a Gaussian Blur applied.

7 **Replace photographs.** Most of the photos in this template use clipping masks. You can replace a photo without breaking the mask. Select a photo, and choose Window > Links. The photo you selected is highlighted. In the Links palette, click the arrow button in the right corner to display the palette menu, and then choose Relink.

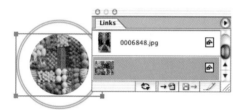

Locate the photograph you want to use, and click Place. Decrease the size if necessary, and drag the photo to center it inside the clipping mask.

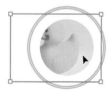

A transparency gives the cover photo a more subtle effect. Place your photo and then choose Window > Transparency and enter an opacity value.

Variation: Use an object blend to create quick graphic elements

1 **Create a shape.** Select the Ellipse tool in the toolbox, press Shift to constrain the shape to a circle, and drag a small shape. With the Selection tool, Alt/Option-drag to duplicate the circle.

2 **Create the object blend.** Color the circles with a selection from the Swatches palette. Select both circles and choose Object > Blend > Blend Options. For Spacing, choose Specified Steps and enter 4; click OK. This value determines the number of circles that will be created between the two selected objects. To set the blend, choose Object > Blend > Make.

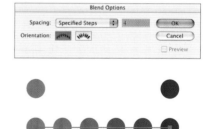

3 **Edit the object blend.** To change the number of steps, choose Object > Blend > Blend Options and enter a new value. This example has two specified steps.

Use OpenType fonts to spice up your artwork and give it a special finish. Illustrator CS ships with many OpenType fonts that you can incorporate into your next project.

Selecting OpenType fonts is a snap when you use the font preview menu. Choose Window > Type > Character and click the Font menu arrow to display your available fonts. OpenType fonts are indicated with a green and black *O* icon. Highlight an OpenType font to reveal the styles included with that font.

Many OpenType fonts include alternative characters sets and features—such as swashes, fractions, ornaments, and ligatures—that let you easily add an elegant flair to your type. To apply an alternate character to an OpenType font, select the type (this example uses Adobe Garamond Pro Italic), choose Window > Type > OpenType and click the corresponding button at the bottom of the palette.

The Frugal Chef

The Frugal Chef

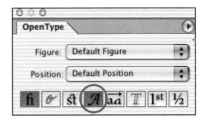

For example, to apply a swash to an individual character, use the Type tool to highlight a character and then click the Swash button.

To enhance this type transformation, select *The* and in the OpenType palette, choose Superscript/ Superior from the Position menu. This example was completed using a recolored version of the Chef symbol (Window > Symbol Libraries > Food).

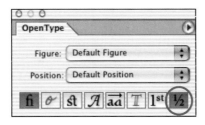

Another great OpenType feature is the ability to format fractions instantly. Enter you text, select it with the Selection tool, and click the Fractions button at the bottom of the OpenType palette. This example also uses the Small Caps feature in the Character palette.

2 1/2 c. flour
1/2 c. milk
1/4 c. butter
1TBSP vanilla

2 ½ c. flour
½ c. milk
¼ c. butter
1 TBSP vanilla

Maximize a Two-Color Design

Whether you use a little color or a lot, Illustrator can help stretch your design budget.

Dreaming of an elaborate four-color print design, but limited by a one or two-color budget? No worries. You may have to skimp on price, by you don't have to compromise on creativity. In this project, you'll work with templates, type ornaments, patterns, swatches, gradients, duotones, brushes—all combined with a few simple techniques. You are certain to find inspiration to tackle your next two-color design.

1 **Open the template.** Save time by using a pre-existing template that already has formatted column markers, crop marks, and text blocks.

Choose File > New from Template > Templates > Marketing > Newsletter 3.ait and click New from Template. This opens a copy of the original template in a new, untitled document. Save and name your new document, and click OK.

2 **Open the color library and plan your color scheme.** Choose Window > Swatch Libraries > Pantone Solid Uncoated.

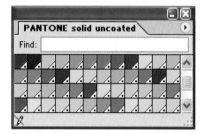

When designing with two colors, you can sometimes achieve a richer look by selecting a complementary color rather than black. If your design has small type, pick a color that is dark enough to make the text readable.

Choose the colors you want to use, and then add them to your document Swatches palette by clicking the color in the Pantone Solid Coated swatch library. Close the swatch library palette when you have finished.

Note: What you see onscreen is an RGB representation of the color. When selecting and working with color, always refer to actual printed examples of your colors.

3 **Delete unwanted elements.** Using the Selection tool, select template elements that won't be part of your new design; then delete them. Not much may remain in the template, but consider the time you saved just in text formatting.

4 **Change the headline text and intial cap.** Using the Selection tool, Shift-click the headlines to select them and, in the Character palette, change the font. The font in this example is from the Charlemagne Std font family, one of many OpenType fonts that ship with Adobe Illustrator CS. In the Swatches palette, select one of your new colors.

To format the initial cap, select the Type tool and double-click to highlight one of the existing letters. In the Character palette, select a new font (this example uses Charlemagne Std Bold), and enter a font size of 150 points. Click the Selection tool, and drag to reposition the letter and eliminate the overlap on the body text.

With the letter still selected, choose Window > Appearance and click the Reduce to Basic Appearance button at the bottom of the palette. You are now ready to recolor the letter.

To recolor the type, use the Selection tool to select the three initial caps, choose Window > Gradient, and drag the gold Pantone swatch from the Swatches palette over the black end of the gradient slider in the Gradient palette. To recolor the body type, click the type, choose Edit > Select All, and select a new color from the Swatches palette.

5 **Add a type ornament.** The space at the top of the newsletter is perfect for a big graphic image. Choose Window > Type > Glyphs. In the Glyphs palette, choose Adobe Caslon Pro from the pop-up menu at the bottom of the palette. From the Font Style menu, choose Semibold Italic. Scroll to the ornaments at the bottom

of the Glyphs palette. Select the Type tool in the toolbox, click in the empty space at the top of the newsletter, and then double-click the ornament in the Glyphs palette. With the Type tool, highlight the ornament and, in the Character palette, enter a new point size; then select a color swatch to recolor the type ornament. In the Color palette, enter a tint of 15% in the Tint Percentage text box. Deselect.

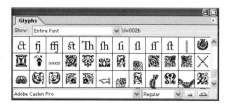

Note: Use the Glyphs palette instead of those frustrating key commands when you want to access alternate characters. In the Glyphs palette, a black triangle in the lower right of the character indicates alternate characters are available; click the triangle to view the choices. OpenType fonts offer the most variety.

6 **Add interest with patterns.** Apply a pattern to add real surface interest to your two-color design. Choose

Window > Swatch Libraries > Other Library > Presets > Patterns > Decorative > Decorative_Ornament.ai and click Open. Drag the Chinese Tiles pattern swatch onto the artboard. With the Direct Selection tool, select the black background and click the gold color swatch to recolor the background; enter a tint of 50% in the Color palette. With the Selection tool, select all of the pattern tile and drag it into the document's Swatches palette. Using the Rectangle tool, draw a shape; click the new pattern swatch in the Swatches palette to fill the shape.

7 **Create a compound shape.** Use the Type tool to create your text. Click the Selection tool to select the text and choose Type > Create Outlines. Place the letters over the shape, Shift-click the patterned shape to add it to the selection, and then choose Object > Compound Shape > Make.

Note: When printing with only one color, take advantage of the negative

and positive areas in a compound shape to give the illusion of a two-color design. When you print a one-color project on colored paper, the paper color will show through the compound shape. To add more interest, add a tint of your color over the negative area of the compound shape.

Ink

Paper

8 **Apply a few brushes.** Brushes let you add a curving, organic quality to your design; you can create many different looks by changing the brush's path direction, bend, and color. Using the Pen tool, draw a simple path, dragging the end point to create a smooth curve. Open the brush libraries by choosing Window > Brush Libraries > Arrows_Special for the arrow brush, and choosing Window > Brush Libraries > Artistic_Watercolor for the watercolor brush. With the curved path selected, select the brush in the library. Increase the stroke weight to thicken the brush effect.

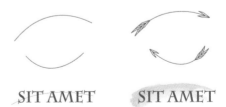

SIT AMET   SIT AMET

9 **Use a duotone for an interesting photographic effect.** You can create a duotone in Adobe Photoshop or place a photo in Illustrator, and choose Filter > Colors > Convert to Grayscale. Be sure to call out the photo placement to your print shop, to have the shop print the photo on one of the Pantone plates. This duotone effect works best with darker colors.

2 **Preview the overprint.** To view your overprint, choose View > Overprint Preview. When working with very dark spot colors, you may want to add a tint before overprinting to avoid a muddy color mix.

Variation: Customize existing two-color designs

1 **Open the template.** Choose File > New from Template > Templates > Marketing > Flyer 3.ait and click New from Template. This opens a copy of the original design template in a new, untitled document. Save and rename your new document.

Variation: Blend artwork by overprinting spot colors

1 **Create the overprint.** Generally, when you print overlapping shapes in spot colors, the top color will knock out the bottom color. Overprinting allows you to blend the colors, giving you even more flexibility when working with a two-color design. First create the shapes or text that you want to overprint. Select the topmost object, choose Window > Attributes, and select Overprint Fill.

2 **Delete unwanted elements.** With the Direct Selection tool, select the building shapes; then Shift-click the type inside the red bar, the red bar, and the address block at the bottom. Delete your selection.

3 **Reshape the cloud.** Select the Ellipse tool (grouped under the Rectangle tool) and drag two circular shapes to the blunt end of the pre-existing cloud shape. Use the Color palette to fill the shapes with white. To create one continuous cloud, Shift-click the two new shapes and the large cloud shape. Choose Window > Pathfinder and click the Merge button.

4 **Rearrange the object layers.** It's easy to reorganize your elements using the Layers palette. Choose Window > Layers and click the gray arrow next to the Artwork layer to display its components. Select the topmost item, the cloud, and drag it between the <Group> banner art grouping and the <Path> gray background element.

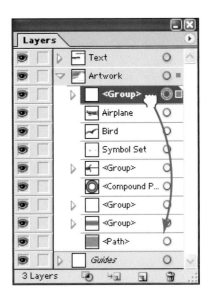

5 **Recolor the art elements.** Choose Window > Swatch Libraries > Pantone Solid Uncoated. You will change all of the red fills at once, but first you must break the airplane symbol instance. With the Selection tool, select the plane in the artwork and, in the Symbols palette, click the Break Link to Symbol button. Click outside the artboard to deselect everything. In the toolbox, select the Direct Selection tool and click the red banner shape. Choose Select > Same > Fill Color and select a new color in the Pantone Solid Uncoated swatch library. Deselect. With the Direct Selection tool, Shift-click the three blue shapes on the airplane; in the Color palette, enter 50% in the Tint Percentage text box.

6 **Recolor the type.** Select the large headline at the top. Choose Window > Appearance and select the stroke; in the Color palette, choose white. Select the fill in the Appearance palette and, in the Swatches palette, click the new Pantone color swatch. In the Appearance palette, select the color of the second fill and, in the Swatches palette, select the new Pantone color swatch. Select the type in the lower left of the design; recolor it and then reposition it closer to the bottom of the flyer.

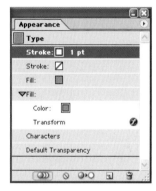

7 **Add a gradient to the sky.** Select the gray background shape and click the new Pantone color swatch in the

Swatches palette to recolor it. With the background still selected, choose Window > Gradient. Drag the blue fill from the Color palette to the Gradient palette, releasing the mouse button over the black end of the gradient slider. In the Gradient palette, enter 90 for the angle. Deselect.

8 **Apply a last-minute color change.** Illustrator makes it so easy to globally change colors, you can produce multiple color options of your artwork, in just minutes. All you have to do is drag a alternate swatch over your original Pantone color swatch.

Note: Keep in mind that when you replace a swatch, the original will be lost. To keep track of the colors you use, make a copy of your original swatch. Select the swatch, and in the Swatches palette, click the arrow pull-down menu and choose Duplicate Swatch. A "1" at the end of the name indicates the swatch is a copy.

To make a global color change, select a new color in the Pantone Solid Uncoated swatch library and Alt/Option-drag the new color over the original swatch (not the copy) in your documents Swatches palette. Every instance of the original color will be replaced with your new selection. Double-click the swatch you just replaced and rename it with the appropriate Pantone number.

To decrease the intensity of a spot color, adjust the tint value in the Color palette—don't change the spot color's transparency. In contrast, you can decrease the intensity of CMYK colors in two ways. You can either decrease equally the amount of cyan, magenta, yellow, and black, or you can add transparency. For either spot or CMYK colors, experiment with the different techniques and then check the color fidelity by converting your file to a PDF file and having your local quick printer print it. A high-quality PDF print is an inexpensive investment, especially compared to a press check. The example shown here uses a pre-existing symbol (Window > Symbol Libraries > Occasions > Column).

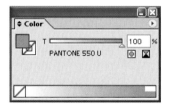

Pantone 550 U: Original spot color and its corresponding Color palette.

Lighter shades created with tint values of Pantone 550 U.

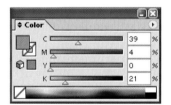

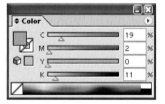

CMYK equivalent of spot color.

Lighter shades created by holding down Ctrl/Command and dragging any of the three C, M or Y color sliders; the sliders will move in tandem. Dragging the sliders to the left lightens the color.

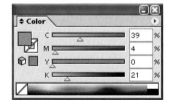

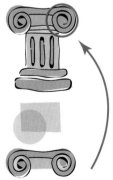

CMYK equivalent of spot color.

Lighter shades created by decreasing the opacity in the Transparency palette. When you decrease the opacity, some shapes may disappear.

Brand Your Documents with Design Elements

Quickly produce graphic design elements to give your business
documents a unique identity.

Illustrator is a great tool for quickly producing graphic design elements that brand and pull together a set of documents. The beauty of Illustrator's vector graphics is that you can modify them in many ways to fit your needs. For this project, you'll use a logo from a template file—and see how easy it is to extract and transform a set of design elements.

1 **Get started.** Choose File > New from Template > Templates > Business Sets > BusSet 1 Business Card.ait and click New from Template. Select the logo in the upper left corner and choose Edit > Copy. Open a new CMYK color mode file and choose Edit > Paste. The logo in this case is a symbol and a compound illustration. You'll break apart the logo and re-create parts of it to complete the design elements.

2 **Prepare the image.** Select and zoom in on the image. Make sure that the Transparency palette is open (Window > Transparency). Enter 30% for the opacity, with Normal selected as the blending mode. Choose Object > Lock > Selection to lock the image. In the View menu, make sure that Show Rulers is checked. Position the pointer on the vertical ruler at the extreme left

and drag a guide to the center of the logo. Drag a guide from the horizontal ruler at the extreme top to the top of the dish half-circle. Choose View > Guides and make sure that Lock Guides is checked.

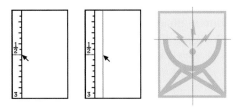

3 **Re-create the logo dish.** In the toolbox, select None for Fill; then click the Stroke button. In the Stroke palette, set the weight to 1 point. Select the Pantone 274U (dark blue) swatch that was placed in the Swatches palette when the image was pasted onto the artboard. Use the Ellipse tool and center its marquee on the intersection of the guides. Hold down both the Alt/Option and Shift keys and drag a circle to the center of the half circle. Deselect the image and use the Direct Selection tool to reselect the circle. Click the top join point and delete it to form the half-circle of the dish. Deselect.

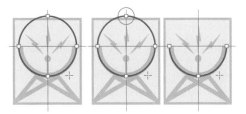

4 **Add the legs.** Select the Pen tool. In the Stroke palette, click the arrow button in the upper right corner to display the palette's options menu and choose Show Options. Click the Round Join option. With the Pen tool, start at the upper left portion of the leg where it meets the dish and draw to the left bottom of the leg; then draw to the upper right edge of the right leg using the dimmed image as your template.

Select the leg. In the toolbox, click the Reflect tool and Alt/Option-click the image's center vertical guide to display the Reflect dialog box. Select Vertical, enter 90° as the Angle value, and click Copy to create the other leg of the dish.

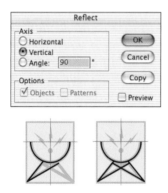

Select all of the stroked lines. In the Stroke palette, increase the Weight value to match the thickness of the dimmed image. Deselect.

5 **Create the center dish elements.** Using the dimmed image as a template, draw the stem of the dish with the Pen tool and size the stroke to match the thickness of the template's stem. With the Ellipse tool, draw the circle at the tip of the stem and fill it with dark blue, no stroke.

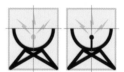

6 **Combine the dish elements.** Select the legs and dish half-circle and choose Object > Path > Outline Stroke to change the lines to fills. Shift-click the circle to add it to the selection. In the Pathfinder palette (choose Window > Pathfinder if it's not open), Alt/Option-click the Add to Shape Area button to combine the dish elements.

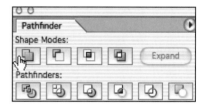

7 **Add the lightning bolts.** Choose Object > Unlock All to unlock and select the dimmed logo. Hold down Alt/Option and drag the image to the right to duplicate the image, and then press Shift to constrain its movement as you place it next to the original. In the Transparency palette, enter 100% for opacity.

To break out the lightning bolts from the logo symbol, it will be necessary to break the symbol link, ungroup the image and then expand the logo elements. With the logo symbol selected, click the Break Link to Symbol button in the Symbols palette.

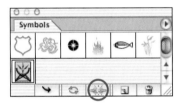

Choose Object > Ungroup twice, to release the nested groups in the compound illustration. Deselect. Select the blue dish graphic and choose Object > Expand Appearance. In the Path-finder palette, click the Divide button (![icon]) and choose Object > Ungroup to release the lightning bolt elements. Deselect. Shift-click the three lightning bolts to select them and group them (Ctrl/Command+G). Press Alt/Option and drag to the left to duplicate the selection and place it over the dimmed lightning bolts. Select and delete the dimmed logo.

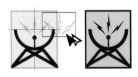

8 **Create your design set graphics.** Select the blue dish with the frame on top of the yellow square and shift-click the lightning bolts group to add them to your selection; then press Ctrl/Command+G to group them. Duplicate the group by holding down Alt/Option and dragging to the right to create the logo without a background. Next select the lightning bolt group in the dish without the frame and duplicate it to the left. Deselect. Select the dish and lightning bolts without the frame and group them.

9 **Copy the design set.** You will now duplicate the design set that you will color in a later step. Select the design set. Copy it by holding down Alt/Option and, while dragging downward, press Shift to constrain its movement and place it directly below the original set. Press Ctrl/Command+D to duplicate it again. Deselect.

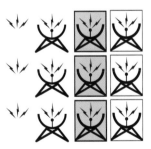

10 **Optimize the Swatches palette.** The logo elements are colored with

Pantone spot colors. You will color some of the design elements white, but first you must change the default white in the Swatches palette from a process color to a spot color. In the Swatches palette, double-click the White swatch to display the Swatch Options dialog box. Choose Spot Color for Color Type and click OK.

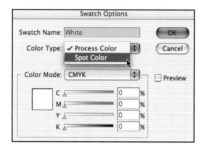

To complete the color set, make a percentage of the spot blue. In the Swatches palette, click the Pantone 274U swatch. In the Color palette, click the arrow button in the upper right corner and choose Show Options if they are not open. Enter 5% and click the Fill box to set the color; then drag the swatch into the Swatches palette to save it.

11 **Simplify the Swatches menu.** When using a limited spot-color palette, it is a good idea to clear out the unused process colors from the Swatches palette. With the Selection tool, click the swatch to the right of the spot white you just created. Shift-click the first swatch to the left of the dark blue Pantone color at the bottom of the palette. All of the in-between swatches now will have a white frame around them. Drag them to the Trash button at the bottom of the palette. The Swatch palette should now have the four spot colors you will use to color the design set.

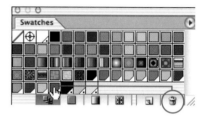

12 **Color the design set.** Start with the two-color logo groups (second from the end in each row). Select the dark blue dish in the second logo from the top and in the Swatches palette, color it yellow. Next select the yellow background of the logo and color it with the dark blue. Deselect. Color the third two-color logo by selecting the blue dish and coloring it white; then select its background and color it with the dark blue. Use the Selection tool on the one-color design elements and color them as shown in the following illustration.

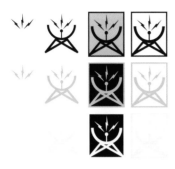

Look at the examples in the Adobe Illustrator CS Templates > Business Set 1 files to see the many variations possible using just two colors and a couple of design elements extracted from the logo. Experiment with the design set and create your own document versions of Business Set 1.

☐ **Variation: Extract colors from an image to brand your documents**

Another excellent technique for branding documents is to extract color from logos or other central images important to a business or project and apply them to design elements and backgrounds.

1   **Get started.** Choose File > New from Template > Templates > Business Sets > BusSet 2 Post Card.ait and click New from Template. Select the center house logo symbol in the top layout and choose Edit > Copy. Open a new CMYK color mode file and choose Edit > Paste. Zoom in on the logo.

2   **Clear the Swatches palette.** Click the first color swatch in the palette, Shift-click the last swatch, and drag all of the swatches to the Trash button at the bottom of the palette (you can't delete the Registration and None swatch).

3   **Sample the colors.** In the toolbox, select the Eyedropper tool. Hold down Shift and click the end of the Eyedropper tool on any part of the image. The color display in the toolbox Fill box changes as you sample around the logo. For this image, choose very light colors that will work as background and accent colors.

Sample pale blue from the roof, pale brown from the front exterior, light yellow from the chimney, pale green of the sky, and light gray from the walkway. As you sample with the Eyedropper tool, look at the toolbox Fill box. When you see the color you

want, drag it from the toolbox Fill
button into the Swatches palette to
save it for your color set.

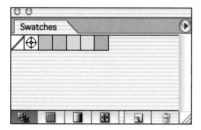

 Note: When color-sampling symbols,
photographs, or bitmaps with the Eyedropper tool, you must hold down the
Shift key.

Look at the Business Set 2 sample
files. All of the documents in the set
were designed using accent and background colors extracted from the logo.
Experiment with sampling other colors from the logo and applying them
to background and design elements.

Make a design set symbol library of artwork that you frequently use.

A symbol library is a file with a set of images made into symbols and saved for later use. Create a symbol library folder on your hard drive where symbol files can be easily stored and found. You can open symbol library files as any Illustrator file, and you can use them as templates for a document set. You can also open symbol files from within any other file. To open a symbol library in another file, choose Window > Swatch Libraries > Other Library, and select and open the file. The design symbols will open as a palette in the file.

Keep your symbol libraries simple. Delete the default symbols in the Symbols palette before you create a new set. Click the first symbol in the palette, Shift-click the last symbol in the palette, and drag all of the symbols to the Trash button at the bottom of the palette. If you want to restore the default symbols, choose Window > Symbols > Default_CMYK or Default_RGB (depending on the color mode of the file in which you are working). To create a symbol for your symbol library, use the Selection tool to drag a design group into the Symbols palette. In the Symbols palette, double-click one of the new images to display the Symbol Options dialog box; name the symbol. Repeat the process with the rest of the images you want in your library.

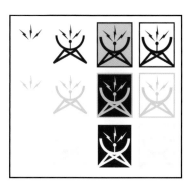
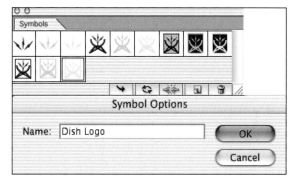

To easily find and use your favorite colors, make a color set into a swatch library.

Create a swatch library folder on your hard drive where you can easily save and find your favorite color sets. To open the swatch library in another file, choose Window > Swatch Libraries > Other Library and select and open the file. The color set will open as a color palette in the file.

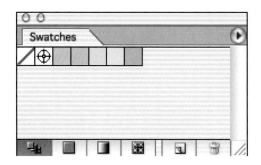

Materials: | **Project 7**

Food Symbol library

Decorative_Objects
Objects_Objects
Decorative_Banners
and Seals
brush libraries

Make a (Type) Statement

Create interesting typographical effects with easy-to-use type tools and effects.

Ready to make a real statement? With Illustrator's versatile type tools, you can easily create dazzling typographic designs. In this project, you will learn to create type along a path, reshape type within an envelope and distort it, and warp type with simple effects. If you're typographically challenged, get inspired by looking through the great examples of different type techniques in the Illustrator CS design templates.

1 **Get started.** Open a new file. Find or create a simple shape to use as the path for your text. To replicate this example, choose Window > Symbol Libraries > Food.

Drag the Escargot symbol from the Food Symbols library onto the artboard. At the bottom of your documents Symbols palette, click the Break Link to Symbol button. With the image still selected, double-click the Scale tool in the toolbox and enter a uniform scale of 250%. Click OK.

2 **Create the path type.** You'll use a copy of the white spiral, that is inside the shell, as the type path. To select only the spiral, select the Direct Selection tool in the toolbox, Alt/Option-click the white spiral shape, and double-click the Scale tool. Enter a uniform scale of 125%. Click OK.

3 **Add the text.** In the toolbox, click the Type tool and drag to the right to select the Path Type tool. Click the top line of the spiral shape (zoom in on the artwork if needed). The cursor will blink when the path is selected. Enter your text.

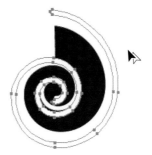

4 **Format and adjust the type.** Using the Selection tool, select the shell and change its fill color so that you can see where the text ends. Select the Path Type tool and change the font family and point size by triple-clicking the text to select all of it, and choosing a new font in the Character palette. Increase or decrease the point size until the text flows to your liking.

You can easily adjust where the type starts and ends. With the Selection tool, select the path type, click the insertion point at the beginning of the type, and drag in the direction you want the type to move.

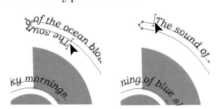

The type moves smoothly along the path. Dragging the path type is a great alternative to entering extra spaces to tweak the type. You can even drag the type around the end of the path or pull the I-beam straight down so that the tops of the characters run along the baseline of the path.

5 **Add a color transition to the type.** A nice word break appears where the text passes over the shell. To add more interest, reverse out this section of type. With the Path Type tool, click where you want the transition to start and then drag to highlight the remaining characters. In the Color palette, select a white fill.

6 **Customize with gradients and subtle color changes.** Make a stock illustration come alive with a new color scheme. To replicate this example of a swirling shell gradient, open the Beach swatch library (Window > Swatch Libraries > Beach). Select the shell shape, choose Window > Gradients, and then drag your choice of beach color swatches individually over the gradient sliders in the Gradient palette.

To add the background gradient, draw a rectangle and fill it with a blue gradient that fades to white. Highlight the type and select a blue swatch from the Beach swatch library.

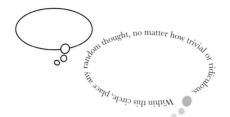

 Create the envelope. Using the Direct Selection tool, select and delete the circle on the birdhouse, and then copy the house shape and paste it elsewhere on your artboard for later use. Use the Type tool to create the number; then select and paste it behind the new shape. Select both the shape and the number and choose Object > Envelope Distort > Make with Top Object. To create a color boundary, bring the enveloped number to the front (Object Arrange > Bring to Front) and drag it over the original birdhouse.

Note: Use an existing shape for your type path. The shape shown here is Text Balloon 2 from the Decorative_Banners and Seals brush library. To create this example, drag the brush from the Decorative_Banners and Seals brush library onto your artboard. Select the Path Type tool and click the oval, just next to the bubbles, and enter your text. Recolor the bubbles for a unique combination of typography and art.

Variation: Use an envelope for a fun hand-lettered look

Simple shapes make great envelope objects, and when combined with a fun typeface, the results are simply unique.

 Recolor the number. You can edit the envelope's content. Select the envelope, choose Object > Envelope Distort > Edit Contents. In the Color palette, choose a white fill.

 Select a shape. To make sure that your type will be readable, select a shape that has a limited number of points. This example uses the Birdhouses brush from the Objects_Objects brush library along with the typeface Giddyup, included in Illustrator CS.

 Stretch the envelope. To further contort the number, select the Direct Selection tool and click the individual points that make up the house shape and drag them until the number's shape is to your liking. In this example, the sides of the house were moved in to crop out the white numbers.

Variation: Create attention–grabbing headlines with a warp

1 **Open the banner art.** Choose Window > Brush Libraries > Decorative_Banners and Seals. Drag the Banner 9 image to your artboard.

▶ **Note:** You can use only the art element by dragging a brush image to your artboard. For more movement, apply this brush to a wavy path.

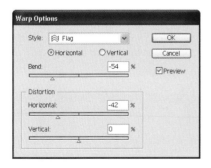

2 **Warp the type.** Create your text and with the Selection tool, click the type and choose Effect > Warp > Flag. To match the curve of the banner art, set Bend to a negative value. Setting Horizontal Distortion to a negative value will make the letters gradually decrease in size.

TOP SELLERS!

3 **Customize the banner image.** Using the Direct Selection tool, click the points on the banner and adjust them to make it more wavy. With the banner still selected, add a gradient. To make the type pop, add a drop shadow (Effect > Stylize > Drop Shadow). To mimic this example, in the Drop Shadow dialog box set the mode to Normal, double-click the color picker, and select white. Reduce the X offset, Y offset and blur to 2 points.

Below are just a few of the warp effects available in Adobe Illustrator.

Warp effect: Rise
Warp effect on fish: Fisheye

Warp effect: Arc

Warp effect: Bulge

The professionally designed templates included in Illustrator CS are packed with great examples of type use. Check out the templates the next time you're looking for a unique type treatment, effect, or style.

Templates > Cards and Postcards > Invitation 2.ait
This example uses the Path Type and Area Type tools and a simple skew for some type perspective.

Templates > CD and DVD > DVD 3 Booklet.ait
This example uses multistroked and filled type and a free distortion (Effect > Distort & Transform > Free Distort).

Templates > Marketing > Newsletter 3.ait
This example integrates a type effect (Effect > Warp > Arc) with an image.

Project 7: Make a (Type) Statement   55

Materials:

*Postcard 1 Blank
template*

Sky gradient library

*Nature
Weather
Artistic Textures
symbol libraries*

Project 8

Design with Symbols

Embellish your next party invitation—or any graphic design—with preset symbols, using Illustrator's versatile Symbol Sprayer tool.

■ It's easy to create hundreds of unique designs using the Symbol Sprayer tool with the symbol libraries. In this project, you will create a party invitation—by spraying, adjusting, tinting, and screening various symbol images. You will also learn how to create your own custom symbol, make a quick map, and texture-spray a photo.

1 **Get started.** This project uses many different resource files. You'll start with the blank postcard template. Choose File > New from Template > Templates > Blanks > Post Card_ Blank.ait and click New from Template. The artboard in this template has two cropped postcards, so that you can easily design the front and back artwork all in one file. Save and rename your file.

2 **Create the gradient backgrounds.** Open the Sky swatch library by choosing Window > Swatch Libraries > Other Library > Gradients > Sky.ai.

▶ **Note:** The default palette view is set at thumbnail. To list the contents of any palette, click the arrow pull-down menu on the palette and choose List View.

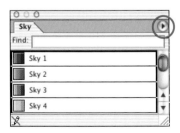

Select the Rectangle tool in the toolbox and drag a rectangle that fills the top two-thirds of the postcard for the sky and another rectangle below it for the water. Select the first rectangle and then select the Sky 19 gradient in the Sky Gradient palette. To adjust the direction of the gradient, choose Window > Gradient, specify a 90° angle, and press Tab to apply the new value.

Now select the water rectangle and select Sky 6 in the Sky Gradient palette. Specify a 90° angle. To mimic the colors in the sky, you need to adjust the gradient color stops. With the water rectangle still selected, choose Show Options from the Gradient palette menu. Click a gradient stop and select a new color in the Color palette; repeat this process for the remaining stops. To move the highlight color closer to the top of the rectangle, select the that color's gradient stop and drag it to the right along the gradient slider.

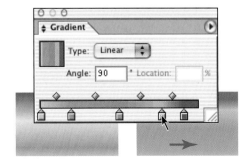

3 **Add Clouds.** Choose Window > Symbol Libraries > Nature. Select the Symbol Sprayer tool in the toolbox and select the Cloud 1 symbol in the Symbols palette.

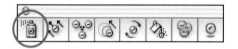

Click the artboard and hold down the mouse button; the longer you hold down the mouse button, the more clouds you'll spray. If you spray too many clouds, hold down the left bracket ([) key to decrease the diameter of the sprayer, and Alt/Option-click to remove the symbol instances. When the diameter of the sprayer is small enough, each time you Alt/Option-click you remove one cloud.

To add a second cloud symbol, select Cloud 2 in the Symbols palette and, with your original symbol set selected, spray the next cloud symbol. Repeat this process with Cloud 3.

To add or delete clouds, select the cloud symbol in the Symbols palette, select the symbol set and Alt/Option-click the sprayer on top of the cloud instance that you want to change.

▷ **Note:** To customize your symbol set more easily, detach the Symbol tools from the toolbox. Simply position the pointer on the Symbol Sprayer tool in the toolbox and drag right to the arrow at the end of the toolbar.

4 **Adjust the placement of the clouds.** With the symbol set still selected, click the Symbol Shifter tool in the toolbox.

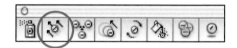

To fine-tune the placement of the clouds, drag the Symbol Shifter tool in the direction you want them to move.

The Symbol Shifter tool also lets you adjust the stacking order of the symbols within a symbol set, for a more realistic and random appearance. In the Symbols palette, select the symbol you want to change. To bring a symbol instance forward in the stacking order, Shift-click the instance; to send a symbol instance backward, hold down Alt/Option and Shift-click the symbol instance.

5 **Make the clouds transparent.** Use the Symbol Screener tool to increase the transparency of the cloud symbols. Double-click the Symbol Screener tool in the toolbox, set the intensity to 3, and click OK. A lower intensity setting lets you apply transparency more gradually.

With the symbol set still selected, click or drag the Symbol Screener tool across the symbol set to increase the transparency; Alt/Option-click to decrease the transparency.

This example consists of three different cloud symbols. To adjust the transparency of a specific cloud, select that symbol in the Symbols palette and click the Symbol Screener tool on top of that symbol instance. To adjust the transparency of the entire symbol set, deselect all symbols in the Symbols palette, select the symbol set, and then use the Symbol Screener tool.

6 **Create the land mass and sandy beach.** Select the Pen tool in the toolbox, click the tool at the horizon, and drag to create the smooth curves at the edge of the land mass. Choose a dark green color in the Color palette.

To create the sandy beach, select the land shape and Alt/Option-drag to duplicate.

In the Color palette, fill the new shape with a light tan color.

To reposition the beach behind the land mass, select the beach shape and choose Object > Arrange > Send Backward. Create an irregular edge on your beach shape by using the Direct Selection tool to pull the individual points closer or farther away.

7 **Add trees and resize them.** Select the Symbol Sprayer tool in the toolbox and select the Trees 1 symbol in the Nature symbol library. Spray the trees across the land mass. The tree symbol is too large for this design and needs to be resized.

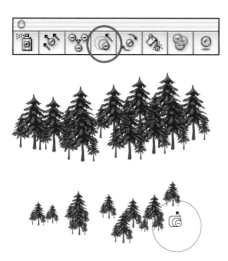

With the symbol set still selected, select the Symbol Sizer tool in the toolbox and Alt/Option-click the tree symbol set to decrease the symbol size. To increase the symbol size, release the Alt/Option key and click the Symbol Sizer tool across the symbol set.

To adjust the spacing, select the Symbol Scruncher tool in the toolbox. With the image still selected, drag the Symbol Scruncher tool across the symbol set.

To fine-tune the spacing, hold down the left bracket ([) key until the diameter of the sprayer is small enough to tweak individual symbol instances.

8 **Create a new symbol.** The trees need something in front to hide the blunt ends of the trunks. Using the Pen or Pencil tool, create a small shrub, and in the Color palette fill the new shape with a green color that complements the trees.

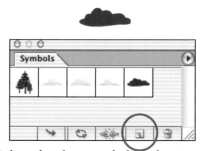

Select the shape and click the New Symbol button at the bottom of the Symbols palette. In the Symbols palette, double-click the new symbol to name it.

Select the Symbol Sprayer tool in the toolbox, and spray the shrub symbol over the bottom of the trees.

10 **Replace the symbol instance.** The best feature of symbols is that they are easy to change and replace. If you had duplicated the shrub image by copying and pasting, you would have had to select each shape before changing the appearance. Using the Symbols palette makes this task a three-second operation. Select your recolored image and Alt/Option-drag over the original symbol in the Symbols palette.

9 **Recolor the new symbol.** To create more contrast between the shrub and the land shape color, you'll recolor the shrub image. Drag the symbol from the Symbols palette onto your artboard.

Click the Break Link to Symbols button at the bottom of the Symbols palette and choose a lighter shade from the Color palette.

When the symbol that you want to replace is highlighted, release the mouse button and the Alt/Option key. All instances of the previous symbol will be replaced. This is an especially handy technique when your artwork contains hundreds of symbol instances.

Note: You can easily lighten or darken the intensity of a CMYK color without resorting to transparency. Select the shape, hold down Ctrl/Command, and click any of the color sliders in the Color palette. As you drag a slider, the other sliders move in tandem. Moving a slider to the left desaturates the color; moving the slider to the right saturates the color.

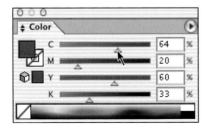

11 **Spray the water ripples with texture.** Using the Symbol tools, you can quickly add texture to your illustration. Choose Window > Symbols Libraries > Artistic Textures and select the Ripples symbol. Select the Symbol Sprayer tool and spray the texture over your image.

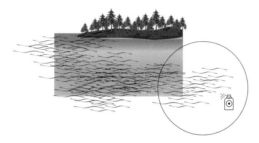

12 **Color-stain the water ripples.** You'll tone down the ripples by adding transparency and staining the ripples purple so that they blend in with the water color. With your image selected, select the Symbol Screener tool and drag it over the Ripples symbol set to add transparency.

Select the Symbol Stainer tool, choose a color in the CMYK color bar at the bottom of the Color palette, and drag the Symbol Stainer tool across the symbol set. In this example the ripples were stained with a dark purple, to blend in with the water colors.

To add more color in one area, hold down the mouse button until the color saturates the image.

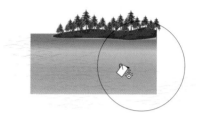

13 **Add highlight ripples.** You'll use the same ripple image, recolor it, and make a new symbol. Drag the Ripples symbol from the Symbols palette onto the artboard and click the Break Link to Symbols button at the bottom of the Symbols palette. Recolor the ripples white; then click the New Symbol button at the bottom of the Symbols palette. With the new symbol selected, select the Symbol Sprayer tool and spray the white Ripples symbol over the water.

Use the Symbol Shifter tool to adjust the placement of the highlight ripples, and use the Symbol Sizer tool to decrease the size of the ripples as they move toward the horizon. Add transparency with the Symbol Screener tool to create the effect of moonlight on the water's surface.

Add the moon symbol. Use the existing symbol libraries to make the job quick and easy. Choose Window > Symbol Libraries > Weather > Phase of Moon 1 and drag the image onto your artboard.

Break the link to the symbol and, in the Color palette, change the fill to white and the stroke to None. To add a hazy effect, with the image still selected, choose Effect > Stylize > Feather. Enter a new radius.

Note: When applying a feather effect, work in small increments and click Preview to view your setting. If you set the feather radius too large, the entire image may disappear.

Create a clipping mask. To complete your design you'll crop the entire image with a clipping mask. Using the Rectangle tool, drag a shape the same size as the postcard template guides. In the Color palette select a fill and stroke of None. Select All (Select > Select All) and choose Object > Clipping Mask > Make.

Variation: Create a quick map

Throwing a party? Your guests will appreciate a simple map.

Draw the roads. Use the Line Segment tool to draw straight roads and the Pen tool to create winding highways.

Add the map symbols. Choose Window > Symbol Libraries > Maps. Drag the symbols you want to use onto your artboard and resize them.

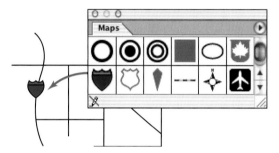

Customize for your location. Add text with the Text tool and position it over the roads and highway symbols.

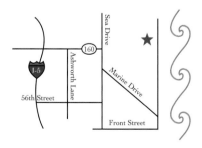

Add landmarks, such as water, using a brush applied to a path. This example uses the Sun Wave in the Borders_Novelty brush library.

Embellish graphic images and wow your audience using preset artistic textures.

When spraying texture with the Symbol Sprayer tool, you may want to adjust the intensity of the sprayer. The lower the intensity, the fewer symbols that will be sprayed, making it easier to control the texture. You can change the settings of any of the symbol tools by double-clicking the tool in the toolbox. In most cases, the default settings were used in the examples throughout this project.

Symbol Libraries > Artistic Textures > Impressionism

Brush Libraries > Decorative_Text Dividers > Text Divider 22

Wine Photo: Applications > Illustrator CS >
Clip Art and Photographs > 0006868

Brush Libraries > Decorative_Celebration > Star Balloon

Symbol Libraries > Artistic Textures > Frosted Beads

Materials:

Metals
Earthtones
gradient libraries

Project 9

Unleash the Power of Gradients

*Create and transform gradients to add dimension
and focus to a project.*

Adding depth to your artwork is easy with Illustrator's gradient libraries and their rich variety of swatches. But you can tap the true power of gradients by knowing how to create new ones and how to modify existing gradients for your particular needs. In this project you will draw a button switch, switch plate, and an indicator light, and bring them to life with gradient fills.

1 **Get started.** Choose File > New. In the New Document dialog box, set Units to Inches and select CMYK for Color Mode and click OK. If the Gradient palette is not open, double-click the Gradient button in the toolbox to display the Gradient palette. If the palette options are not displayed, click the upper-right arrow button and choose Show Options from the palette menu. Select the Stroke button in the toolbox and set the stroke to None by clicking None (☐). Click the Fill button in the toolbox to make the Fill active; then click the White, Black linear gradient in the Swatches palette.

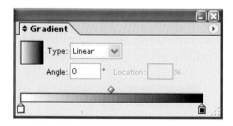

2 **Modify the gradient.** In the toolbox, select the Rectangle tool and click it on the artboard. In the Rectangle

dialog box, enter 4 inches for Width and 5 inches for Height and click OK.

Make sure that the gradient is still selected. Then click the Night Blue swatch in the Swatches palette and drag it to the black square (the stop) below the gradient slider in the Gradient palette to change its color.

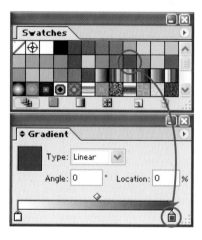

Click the blue gradient stop and duplicate it by holding down Alt/Option and dragging to the left. Repeat this process two more times. Now click the white gradient stop below the gradient slider and Alt/Option-click the Night Blue swatch in the Swatches palette. Your Gradient palette should resemble the illustration on the following page.

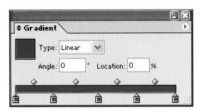

3 **Create the gradient colors.** In the Gradient palette, click the left stop; in the Color palette, enter 22 for C and 11 for M. Click the middle stop; in the Color palette, enter 50 for K. Click the second stop from the right; in the Color palette, enter 40 for C and 20 for M.

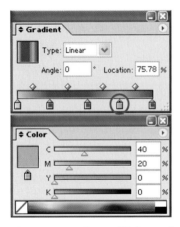

Drag the new gradient fill from the Gradient palette into the Swatches palette to save it.

4 **Create a bevel for the switch plate.** Select the rectangle that you drew in

step 2. To create the bevel, choose Object > Path > Offset Path. In the Offset Path dialog box, enter –0.15 inches for Offset; click OK. You now have two rectangles, one slightly smaller on top of the other.

5 **Transform the gradient to give the bevel depth.** Select the outermost rectangle. In the toolbox, click the Gradient tool and drag its pointer vertically from the top of the image to its bottom. In the Gradient palette, click the far right stop and delete it by dragging it down and out of the palette. Repeat the process to delete the next stop on the right from the palette.

Click the dark blue stop and drag it to the extreme right of the slider bar. Select the middle stop and move it to the middle of the slider.

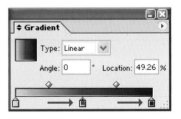

6 **Complete the switch plate bevel.**
Select the inside rectangle. Select the
Gradient tool and drag its pointer
from the top left of the image diago-
nally to the bottom right. Select
both rectangles, group them (Ctrl/
Command+Shift+G), and lock them
(Ctrl/Command+2).

7 **Create the button switch.** Choose
Window > Swatch Libraries > Other
Library > Presets > Gradients >
Metals.ai and click Open. The Metals gradient palette will open in your
file. In the toolbox, select the Ellipse
tool, and in the Metals palette, click
the Blue Steel swatch for the fill. Visu-
ally center the Ellipse tool pointer in
the center of the rectangle. Press Alt/
Option+Shift and draw a circle about
one-half the width of the rectangle.

8 **Add depth to the button switch.**
Make sure that the circle is selected

and choose Object > Path > Offset
Path. In the Offset Path dialog box,
enter –0.15 inches for Offset and click
OK. Select the outer circle. In the
toolbox, click the Stroke button; in the
Color palette, click black; and in the
Stroke palette, enter 3 pt for Weight.
In the toolbox, click the Gradient tool.
Place it at the top of the rectangle
and drag to the bottom of the circle to
change the gradient orientation. Next,
select the inner circle. In the Gradient palette, enter 90° for Angle. Select
both circles and group them.

9 **Create the indicator light.** With the
button switch you just created still
selected, copy it (Ctrl/Command+C).
Choose Edit > Paste in Front to place
it over the original button switch (you
won't see a difference yet). Reduce its
size by choosing Object > Transform >
Scale. In the Scale dialog box Uniform option, enter 30%, and click OK.

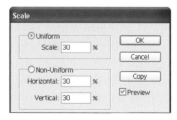

Drag the resized object below the button switch. Deselect the object.

12 **Align the switch elements.** Unlock the switch plate (Ctrl/Command+Alt/Option+2). Select all of the images (Ctrl/Command+A). In the Align palette, click the Horizontal Align Center option to complete the design.

10 **Color the light.** In the toolbox, click the Fill button. With the Group Selection tool, click the indicator light's center circle. In the Swatches palette, select the New Leaf radial swatch. In the Gradient palette, click the right stop, and in the Swatches palette, Alt/Option-click the Red swatch. In the Gradient palette, select the middle stop, and Alt/Option-click the Orange swatch. Select the left stop, and Alt/Option-click the Yellow swatch to complete the light.

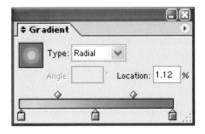

11 **Fine-tune the light.** With the Group Selection tool, click the black outer ring of the indicator light. In the toolbox, click the Stroke button, and in the Stroke palette, enter 1 pt for Weight to reduce the stroke size.

☐ **Variation: Control gradient direction and manipulate color with gradient meshes**

Gradients can be expanded into gradient meshes. Gradient meshes give you control over gradient direction, color, and even shape. By recoloring and moving the mesh points that make up gradient meshes, you can powerfully control an object's appearance.

1 **Get started.** In the toolbox, select the Rectangle tool, and in the Swatches palette, click the Steel Cylinder swatch for the fill and set the Stroke to None. Draw a rectangle on the

artboard. Choose Object > Expand, and in the Expand dialog box, click Gradient Mesh for the Expand Gradient To option. Click OK.

2 **Make the gradient flow within a shape.** Select the Direct Selection tool and drag its marquee over the top of the image to select all of the top anchor and mesh points. In the toolbox, choose the Scale tool and drag from the right to the left until the object resembles the following illustration. Deselect the object. Note that the gradient lines now conform to the direction of the shape.

3 **Add color.** With the Group Selection tool, click the edge of the design to select the image's bounding box (added when the gradient was expanded). Delete it. Select the Direct Selection tool and click inside the image; then click one of the mesh points at the top or bottom of the image. Select any solid color in the Swatches palette and note the color change in the image. Click other mesh points and change their colors to your liking. You can also change color by dragging a color from the Color palette over a mesh point or patch and releasing the mouse button.

☐ **Variation: Experiment with complex gradients and gradient meshes**

1 **Get started.** Choose File > New from Template > Sample Files > Sample Art > Tech Wars.ai and click New from Template.

2 **Select gradients and gradient meshes in the illustration.** Use the gradient palette and the Appearance palette to observe how the gradients were constructed. To see how gradient meshes

were built, use the Direct Selection
tool; click the mesh points and observe
in the Appearance palette the fill colors used.

3 **Change gradient and mesh colors.**
Select gradients in the illustration and
change their color attributes using
the techniques described in steps 2, 3,
and 5 in this project. Experiment with
the gradient meshes in the illustration by changing their color attributes
as explained in steps 2 and 3 of the
previous variation, "Control gradient
direction and manipulate color with
gradient meshes."

An impressive selection of gradient libraries is available in the Illustrator CS application folder. Use these libraries as they are or, with a few easy steps, transform them for your needs.

Create an invitation. Select the Rainbow swatch in the default Swatches palette. Select the Rectangle tool and draw a square in the artwork. In the Transparency palette enter 10 for Opacity, and in the Gradient palette, select Radial from the Type menu—instant background! Add text and design elements to complete your invitation.

Create a background for a Web site banner. Choose Window > Swatch Libraries > Other Library > Presets > Gradients > Metals.ai and click Open. Click Colored Chrome in the Metals palette and with the Rectangle tool, draw a long, narrow, horizontal rectangle on the artboard. Make sure that the image is selected. In the toolbox, select the Gradient tool, and drag a short distance from the left edge, left to right and slightly diagonally, until the design looks something like the following illustration.

Quickly create an alien scene. Choose Window > Swatch Libraries > Other Library > Presets > Gradients > Earthtones.ai and click Open. Click Earthtone 32 in the Earthtones palette. With the Rectangle tool, draw a rectangle on the artboard. Select the Gradient tool. Shift-click and then drag from the top of the image to the bottom. Deselect the rectangle. Select Earthtone 29 Radial in the Earthtones palette, and with the Ellipse tool draw a circle in the upper left-half of the rectangle. Adjust the circle's center point with the Gradient tool. Draw a smaller circle next to the larger one, and fill it with the Earthtone 19 Radial swatch, and adjust it with the Gradient tool. In the toolbox, select the Flare tool and

Alt/Option-click to the right of the background's center. Choose Object > Transform > Scale. In the Scale dialog box, enter a value for Uniform, to scale the flare inside of the rectangle.

Materials:

*Foliage_Floral
brush library*

Arrows symbol library

Make Simple Shapes Blossom

*Create impressive illustrations with the Blend tool and the brush
and symbol libraries.*

Whether you're a novice or an expert illustrator, you can give your project real punch using the Illustrator symbol and brush libraries. The libraries are filled with hundreds of illustrations that you can easily edit to suit your needs. The following project starts with Violets from the Floral Brush library and uses the Blend tool to transform it into a fantasy flower.

1 **Get started.** Open a new file in the CMYK color mode. Choose Window > Brush Libraries > Foliage_Floral. In the Foliage_Floral Brush palette, select Violets and drag it onto your artboard.

2 **Simplify the image.** You need to deconstruct the illustration to its basic elements. With the art selected, choose Object > Ungroup to ungroup the art. Deselect the flowers. Choose the Selection tool, drag the tool into the background of the flower group to select the invisible bounding box, and delete the box. Select the illustration by dragging the Selection tool over the entire image; ungroup it one more time (Object > Ungroup). Deselect the art.

Next, zoom in on any petal. In the toolbox, choose the Group Selection tool. You want to preserve two parts of each petal: the outermost segment and the innermost segment. Double-click any petal to select all of its segments. Hold down Shift and click the outer and inner segments with the Group Selection tool to deselect them. Delete the selections that remain. Repeat this process with each petal until you are left with a basic illustration from which you will create the new flower.

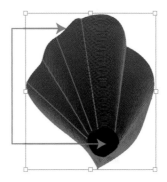

3 **Apply the Blend tool.** Make sure that your flowers are deselected (Ctrl/Command+Shift+A). In the toolbox, click the Blend tool. If the tool icon is not visible, drag from the Auto Trace tool to the right to select the Blend tool. Double-click the tool or Alt/Option-click your artwork to display the Blend Options dialog box. In the Spacing menu, choose Specified Steps, enter 20, click the Align to Path Orientation option, and click OK.

With the Blend tool, click inside the inner and outer segments of a petal. Deselect the petal by Ctrl/Command-clicking outside your image; then, with the Blend tool, click inside the inner and outer segments of the next petal to blend the shapes. Continue deselecting and blending the inner and outer petal segments until you've blended all of the petals. Your flower group should now resemble a slightly rougher version of the original art you selected from the Foliage_Floral brush library.

4 **Color the Petals.** With the Group Selection tool, Shift-click the outer edge of each petal to select them all. In the Swatches palette, click the Steel Cylinder swatch. Deselect the image. Now use the Group Selection tool to Shift-click the inner segment of each

petal until all are selected. Select the Vega Blue swatch from the Swatches palette.

5 **Finish the fantasy flower.** Select and delete the light yellow center shape in each flower. Choose Window > Swatch Libraries > Other Library > Presets > Gradients > Gems and Jewels. Click the Pearl radial fill, select the Ellipse tool, and draw new centers for the flowers. Select the Gradient tool and play with its effects on the applied colors.

Experiment with different colors (remember to always select either the inner or outer segment when applying color). Use the Gradient tool to get different gradient orientations. With the Group Selection tool, drag an outer or inner petal segment to a different location on the artboard for a dramatic result.

Variation: Create gradients from solid colors with the Smooth Color option

1 | **Get started.** Select the Orchid brush in the Foliage_Floral brush library and drag it onto the artboard. Because it was created with only a few specified steps, the orchid group has a very rough appearance. Applying the Smooth Color option of the Blend tool will make it a much richer illustration.

2 | **Simplify the image.** Follow the procedures described in step 2 of the main project to delete the inner segments of the orchid petals and orchid centers.

3 | **Replace colors.** With the Group Selection tool, select one of the pale yellow petal segments. Choose Select > Same > Fill Color. In the Swatches palette, click the Magenta swatch. Deselect the group. With the Group Selection tool, choose one of the dark yellow-brown petal segments. Again choose Select > Same > Fill Color. In the Swatches palette, choose Baby Pink. Color the bent under-petals Baby Pink. They were colored differently than the inner and outer petal segments and would not have been selected using the Select > Same > Fill Color command.

4 | **Blend the colors.** Double-click the Blend tool to display the dialog box. Choose Smooth Color from the Spacing menu, click the Align to Path Orientation option, and click OK.

Deselect the group. Select the Blend tool and click the two new colors of any petal to blend them. Deselect by first pressing down and then releasing Ctrl/Command+Shift+A (this deselects the object and keeps the Blend tool active); then with the Blend tool, click the next two new colors of any petal to blend them.

Repeat this process until all of the petals have been blended. Blend the center of the petal to resemble the following illustration or experiment with your own color choices.

To change the color relationships, select any one of the petal's inner or outer color segments and choose a new solid color.

You can create endless variations of blends and gradients when you combine the Blend tool with other tools and effects. Here are some samples to inspire you.

Create a blue and a red rectangle. Spread them, make one smaller, and apply a step blend.

Choose Window > Symbol Libraries > Arrows and drag Arrow 4 onto the artboard. Break the symbol and duplicate it. Spread the objects, color them, and make one larger. Apply a 10-step blend and choose Object > Envelope Distort > Make with Warp, and experiment with different settings.

Experiment with basic shapes and Blend tool options to create complex-looking illustrations. Draw smaller shapes on top of larger ones and experiment with the Smooth Color option and effects. Remember to use only solid colors with the Smooth Color option.

Using Object > Path > Offset Path with a negative value, create two stars on top of a larger star and blend them with the Smooth color option.

Choose Effect > Distort & Transform > Twist. Enter a numerical value in Angle to distort the outermost shape; then recolor it.

Drag out the center with the Group selection tool, add a 0.1-point stroke, and play with colors.

Morph type. Create two different letters in two different fonts, change them to outlines, and apply the Specified Step option of the Blend tool.

*Invitation 1
template*

*Default_CMYK
swatches*

*Objects
Decorative_
Modern Color
pattern libraries*

■ **Project 11**

Punch-up Projects with Patterns

*The Adobe Illustrator pattern libraries provide a rich variety
of designs. You can easily transform them to fit your needs.*

Practically any vector graphic can be turned into an Illustrator pattern. That makes patterns a powerful and versatile tool for illustrators and designers. But if you are not a skilled practitioner, the Illustrator pattern libraries are for you. The many theme libraries can easily be modified to fit your needs. In this project, you will use patterns to modify a generic Adobe Illustrator template, turning it into a splashy party invitation.

1 **Get started.** Choose File > New from Template. In the New from Template dialog box, choose Templates > Cards and Post Cards > Invitation 1.ait and click New from Template. Save and rename the file.

2 **Open a pattern library.** Choose Window > Swatch Libraries > Other Library > Presets > Patterns > Objects > Objects.ai and click Open. The Objects pattern library will open inside your file.

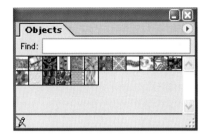

3 **Replace and add patterns.** With the Selection tool, click the invitation's top horizontal pattern. Change its current pattern fill by selecting Balloons in the Objects pattern palette.

Next, you'll change the green background gradient. Choose Window > Swatch Libraries > Default_ CMYK. In the Default_CMYK palette, click the arrow button to display the palette menu and choose List View. Next, select the large green background gradient and change its color by selecting the Sensual Red gradient in the Default_CMYK swatches palette. Click the Gradient tool and Shift-drag its pointer from the bottom of the selection to the top to change the direction of the gradient. You'll layer a pattern on top of this gradient. Copy the selection (Ctrl/Command+C) and paste it in front of itself (Edit > Paste in Front). Select Rainbow Stars in the Objects pattern palette. Replace the left vertical raindrop pattern in the invitation by selecting the pattern in the artwork and change it by clicking Party Favors in the Objects pattern palette.

4 **Modify the patterns.** In the Swatches palette, drag the Balloons pattern swatch onto an empty area of the artboard. Deselect. With the Group Selection tool, click the pattern tile's orange-colored background.

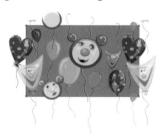

Change its color by clicking the Vega Blue swatch in the Default_CMYK swatches palette. Click the Gradient tool and Shift-drag its pointer from the bottom of the selection to the top. Deselect. Select the pattern tile with the Selection tool. Alt/Option-drag the modified pattern tile on top of the old Balloons pattern swatch in the Swatches palette. The Balloons pattern in the invitation is updated. Delete the Balloons pattern tile from the artboard.

5 **Scale a pattern.** Drag the Rainbow Stars pattern swatch from the Swatches palette onto the artboard. Choose Object > Transform > Scale and enter 70% Uniform Scale and click OK. Alt/Option-drag the pattern tile over the old Rainbow Stars pattern swatch in the Swatches palette and note the scale change in the artwork. Delete the Rainbow Stars pattern tile from the artboard. Select the Rainbow Stars pattern in the design and, in the Transparency palette, specify 40% opacity.

6 **Change the banner text.** Using the Selection tool, delete the address line in the lower left corner, the text *Your Company Name,* and the crown logo from the invitation. Next, select the text *Lorem Ipsum Dolor!* You'll remove the distortion and color from the type, revise the text, and change its pattern. In the Appearance palette, select Free Distort and drag it to the palette's Trash button; then select the red fill and drag it to the Trash button. Select the Type tool and triple-click the text to highlight it. Type *PARTY TIME!* Click the Selection tool. In the Character palette, enter 30 for the font size and 100 for tracking.

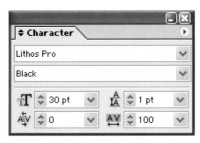

To change the text's pattern, click the blue pattern fill in the Appearance palette; then select Area Rug pattern in the Default_CMYK swatches palette.

7 **Change the body text.** Select the Type tool. Double-click the text *Diam* and type *What:.* Repeat the process: type *When:* for *Amet,* and type *Where:* for *Dolor.* Triple-click *Lorem ipsum dolor sit amet* and type *Be there or be square!*

Click the Selection tool and, in the Swatches palette, change the text fill to white.

8 **Finish the design.** Select the translucent violet-colored rectangle in the invitation and, in the Transparency palette, change the opacity to 100%. In the Default_CMYK swatches palette, change the fill to Lime. To move the lime rectangle behind the party banner, press Ctrl/Command+X to copy the shape to the clipboard. Select the white banner under *PARTY TIME!* and choose Edit > Paste in Back. Click the text *What:* to select its text group and then change its fill to Plum in the Default_CMYK swatches palette.

Open another pattern library and experiment on your design with the techniques you have learned in this lesson.

☐ **Variation: Make a cover insert for a CD case**

1 **Get started.** Open a new file (File > New). In the New Document dialog box, select Inches for Units and CMYK for Color Mode; then click

OK. Choose Window > Swatch Libraries > Other Library > Presets > Patterns > Objects > Objects.ai and click Open

2 **Draw the cover.** Select the Rectangle tool and click its marquee on the artboard. In the Rectangle dialog box, enter 4.75 inches for Width and 4.75 inches for Height; then click OK. Fill the square with Sensual Red with no stroke. Select the Gradient tool and Shift-drag from the bottom of the square to the top. Copy the image (Ctrl/Command+C) and paste it in front (Edit > Paste in Front). Fill the square with the CD pattern in the Objects pattern palette.

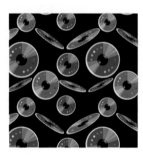

3 **Modify the pattern.** Drag the CD pattern swatch from the Swatches palette onto the artboard. Deselect. With the Group Selection tool, select and color several of the CD label segments to your liking. Then with the Group Selection tool, click the black background in the CD tile, and delete it. Deselect. With the Selection tool, click the CD tile and Alt/Option-drag it over the old CD pattern swatch in the Swatches palette.

Delete the tile from the artboard.

4 **Add a text box.** Select the Rectangle tool and click the tool on the artboard. In the Rectangle dialog box, enter 4.75 inches for width and 0.75 inches for height. In the Swatches palette, click Custard. Select all of the art (Ctrl/Command+A), and in the Align palette, click Horizontal Align Center and Vertical Align Bottom. Add text if you like.

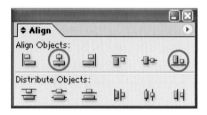

You can easily make a new pattern by adding and reorienting existing pattern elements.

Choose Window > Swatch Libraries > Other Library and, in the pop-up menu, navigate to the Adobe Illustrator CS application folder. Choose Presets > Patterns > Decorative > Decorative_Modern Color.ai. In the Decorative_Modern Color library palette, drag Optical Ovals onto the artboard. With the Group Selection tool, click any one of the blue-colored segments. Choose Select > Same > Fill Color. Choose Edit > Copy and then Edit > Paste in Front. Choose Object > Transform > Rotate and, in the Rotate Options dialog box, enter 90° for Angle. Change the selection's color to Night Blue. Deselect the segments. With the Selection tool, click the pattern tile and drag it into the Swatches palette to create the new pattern. Draw a shape and fill it with the new pattern. If you don't like the colors, drag the pattern swatch onto the art board; then select elements in the pattern tile and change them to your liking. Alt/Option-drag the changed pattern tile over the old one in the Swatches palette to update it.

Experiment with the pattern libraries. By transforming patterns, you can create many useful variations. Save them in a library. Learn to make your own patterns. To learn about constructing patterns and making libraries, see the *Adobe Illustrator CS User Guide*.

Add an Artistic Edge

Create the effect of a colored-pencil rendering with the Scribble effect.

■ To add a casual hand-drawn look to your artwork, use multilayered scribbles to mimic colored-pencil renderings. You can add shaded depth with gradient fills and transparency and even use a scribbled clipping mask. You don't have to be a fine artist to master this technique, all you need is some patience and a good illustration created with basic shapes. For this project, you will use the Fish 2 symbol from the Nature symbol library.

1 **Compose a multilayer Scribble effect.** In this project, you will apply multiple fills and Scribble effects to a single shape using the Appearance palette. In the following illustration, notice how three separate fills, each with a different Scribble effect, make up the scribbled body shape of the fish. To replicate this effect, use a loose spacing setting on the middle layer to let the blue background show through.

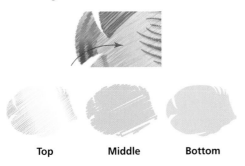

| Top | Middle | Bottom |

Add more layered scribble fills to make the blending effect on the fish body more realistic.

2 **Get started.** Open a new file. Choose Window > Symbol Libraries > Nature. Drag the Fish 2 symbol to your artboard. With the symbol selected, choose Window > Symbols; click the Break Link to Symbol button at the bottom of the palette. With the Direct Selection tool, select and delete the dark blue shape in the very back.

3 **Create the bottom scribble fill.** When building layers, it's best to start with the fill on the bottom and work your way to the top. Start by selecting the body shape with the Direct Selection tool; then choose Window > Appearance and in the Appearance palette, select Fill. In the Color palette, select a light blue color.

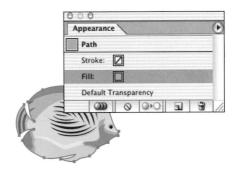

With the body shape still selected, choose Effect > Stylize > Scribble and enter your settings.

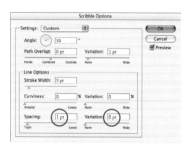

To make an almost solid background with a scribbled edge, set the Scribble effect for the bottom layer with tight, no variation spacing and a thick stroke (3 point). These tight settings work best for placing an illustration on a very dark background.

4 **Create the middle scribble fill.** Next, you'll add a layer mostly for color. It has a smaller stroke setting, wider curviness variation, and a very loose spacing with a lot of variation. In the Appearance palette, select the fill set you created for the bottom layer; then click the arrow button and choose Duplicate Item from the palette menu. This duplicates the fill and the scribble. Select the new fill color in the Appearance palette and select a light green color in the Color palette.

Double-click the Scribble attribute for the new fill and change the settings.

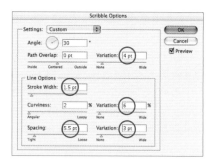

Note: The stroke width in the Scribble Options dialog box refers to the thickness of the lines in the scribbled fill. Think of it as the thickness of your colored-pencil lead. You can set the stroke width very thin to resemble a quill pen or thick for a pastel crayon.

5 **Create the top scribble fill.** To complete the scribble, you'll add a texture layer. In the Appearance palette, select the fill set created for the middle layer; then choose Duplicate Item from the palette menu. Select the new fill color in the Appearance palette and select a light yellow in the Color palette. Double-click the Scribble attribute of the new fill and change the settings.

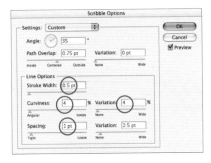

To adjust the texture, make the detail finer by decreasing the scribble stroke (here, to 0.5 pt). Adjust the Path Overlay slightly, add more curviness and tighten the spacing to add surface interest when the gradient fill is applied. Also vary the angle from that of the other two layers. Changing the angle just 5 degrees on your individual scribble fills adds an irregular look, further enhancing the hand-drawn effect.

This same multilayered scribble technique was used to create the dorsal and tail fins. These shapes have two scribbled fills applied to them.

The top fill has loose spacing, 10% (loopy) curviness, and 9% variation.

☐ **Variation: Create realistic shading effects with gradient fills**

1 **Create a custom gradient fill.** Using the Color palette in combination with the Gradient palette makes building gradients quick and easy.

With the body shape selected, in the Appearance palette, select the light yellow top layer fill. Choose Window > Gradient; if the color slider isn't visible, click the arrow button and choose Show Options from the palette menu. Click the yellow fill in the Color palette and drag it to the middle of the gradient slider.

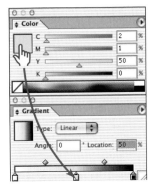

To replace the black gradient stop (the square beneath the slider marking the color change) with light blue, select a light blue fill in the Color palette, drag it over the black gradient stop, and release. To adjust the position of the white color, click the white gradient stop beneath the gradient slider, and drag it to between the blue and yellow stops beneath the slider.

To add another blue stop, Alt/Option-drag the blue color stop to the end of the gradient slider in the Gradient palette to duplicate the stop. Click beneath the gradient slider to add an extra stop. Select a new color in the Color palette. In this example, a light green color color stop was added.

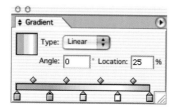

2 **Change the direction of the gradient.** To change the direction of the gradient, select the body shape and enter an angle in the Gradient palette. To adjust the gradient color flow, select the Gradient tool in the toolbox and, with the shape selected, drag the tool in the direction you want it applied.

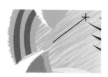

For realistic shading, use the Gradient tool to adjust the gradient fill direction to match the angle of the Scribble effect.

Note: As an alternative to creating your own gradient fill, select from hundreds of preset gradients by choosing Window > Swatch Libraries > Other Library > Presets > Gradients.

□ **Variation: Add dimension with transparency**

You can add even more depth and interest by applying a transparency setting to the gradient fill. This fin shape has an 85% opacity setting— just enough to create an interesting modeling effect.

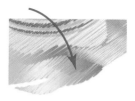

1 **Apply the transparency setting.** With your shape still selected, in the Appearance palette, select the gradient fill, and choose Window > Transparency. Enter a new opacity value.

2 **Create a style.** It takes time to create multilayered scribbles with applied gradients and transparency. Take a minute to save them as styles for future use. Simply select the shape that has the applied effects you want to save; then click the New Style button at the bottom of the Styles palette (Window > Graphic Styles). Double-click the new style to rename it.

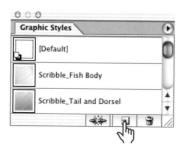

For this fun effect, all you need are a simple shape and a photograph.

Draw or import the shape you want to use as your clipping mask. Select the shape and choose Effect > Stylize > Scribble. Enter your settings and click OK.

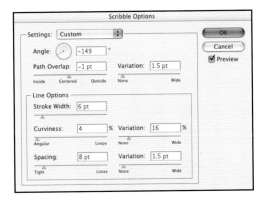

Save the live Scribble effect by creating a style from it. With the shape selected, choose Window > Graphic Styles and click the New Style button at the bottom of the Graphic Styles palette.

With the shape still selected, choose Object > Expand Appearance. Expanding the appearance will discard all of the scribble settings. Now choose Object > Path > Outline Stroke. In the Color palette, choose no fill and no stroke.

To place your photo, choose File > Place. Locate your photo and click Place. Choose Object > Arrange > Send to Back.

To clip the photo, select the shape and the photo and choose Object > Clipping Mask > Make. Using the Direct Selection tool, center your photo behind your clipping mask. To create even more graphic interest, add a colored shape behind the photo and mask.

This technique for creating a scribbled photo mask seems to work best if you use a loopy (high) curviness setting (the percentage of loop as the scribble changes direction) and a thick stroke width.

Materials:

Textures
graphic styles library

Foliage_Leaves
Foliage_Flowers
brush libraries

▊ **Project 13**

Texturize Anything

Create hundreds of different captivating textures with
Illustrator's preset styles and powerful filters and effects.

■ Creating surface textures and applying photographic effects—image enhancements that once seemed possible only in Adobe Photoshop—are now a snap in Illustrator. In this project, you'll learn how to apply a preset texture to type and customize the texture. You'll also apply a filter to a photograph, use a mezzotint overlay, and create an abstract painterly quality with a pointillize effect.

1 **Get started.** Open a new file using RGB color mode. The Graphic Styles libraries contain both RGB and CMYK styles, for use in each respective color mode. RGB styles work best for on-screen display. To change the color mode of an existing document, choose File > Document Color Mode > RGB Color.

2 **Create the text and apply the preset style.** Select the Type tool and enter your text. Most of the texture styles work best on a thick typeface. When you have finished entering the text, click the Selection tool to select the type object. Styles and effects can be applied directly to type, without the need to create outlines. Choose Window > Graphic Styles Libraries > Textures and click RGB Stucco.

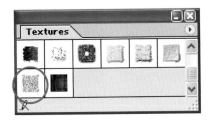

○ **Note:** When applying styles to text, always use the Selection tool to select the type object. Selecting the text with the Type tool will create undesirable results.

3 **Customize the image with additional effects.** First, you will add a craquelure effect and then a drop shadow. With the type still selected, choose Effect > Texture > Craquelure.

Enhance the effect with a drop shadow. With the type selected, choose Effect > Stylize > Drop Shadow. For a more subtle shadow, double-click the color, select a brown tone from the color picker, and click OK.

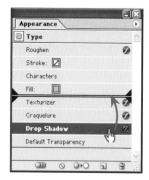

Note: The Appearance palette lists the effects in the order in which they were applied; it is often necessary to adjust the stacking order. Just click an attribute, drag it to a new location, and release the mouse button when you see the arrow bracket. If you are working with a grouped object, the Appearance palette will display the group as Contents. Double-click the word Contents to view the object's appearance attributes.

Variation: Try your hand at creating awesome photographic effects

1 **Get started.** Open a new or existing file using either CMYK or RGB color mode. Illustrator has many filters and effects. Filter menu commands apply to bitmap images only, permanently change the image, and embed it in the document. In contrast, Effect menu commands apply to bitmap images and vector graphics, and are live effects that don't alter the image. To change the settings for an

effect, choose Window > Appearance, double-click the effect attribute in the Appearance palette, enter the setting, and click OK.

2 **Apply a filter.** Applying filters to photographs couldn't be easier. Place your photograph by choosing File > Place. With the photograph selected, choose Filter and then select the filter you want to use. Below are just a few examples of the filters available in Illustrator.

Original photo

Filter > Texture > Grain

Filter > Sketch > Water Paper

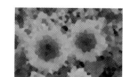

Filter > Pixelate > Crystalize

Filter > Brush Strokes > Crosshatch

Filter > Artistic > Dry Brush   Filter > Artistic > Cutout

Variation: Use a Pixelate effect for some of the most versatile textures

1 **Apply a mezzotint effect to a photograph.** Place a photo. Select the photo, choose Effect > Pixelate > Mezzotint, choose a mezzotint to apply and click OK. The mezzotint effect simulates a print created from an engraved metal plate. This example uses the Long Stroke setting.

The initial effect is very graphic and bold. For an interesting fabric quality, add transparency. Choose Window > Transparency and enter an opacity value (the example here uses a 40% value).

2 **Apply multiple mezzotint effects to create a handmade paper texture.** To give an illustration a layered texture look, add more than one mezzotint effect. Select your shape, in the Appearance palette select the Fill, and choose Effect > Pixelate > Mezzotint. Click OK. With the Fill still selected, enter an Opacity value in the Transparency palette. The smaller the value, the more delicate the effect. A transparency of 10% or less creates a more subtle texture. To layer a second mezzotint texture on top of the first, in the

Appearance palette select the Fill set and choose Duplicate Item from the palette menu.

Change the fill color in the Color palette and then double-click the mezzotint effect to change its type. The yellow leaf has two fills—one fill with a coarse dot mezzotint and a second fill with a grainy dot mezzotint. The green leaf has one fill with two mezzotint effects applied to it, in front of a second, solid fill with no effect. You can make the surface texture more interesting by combining different fills with multiple mezzotint effects.

3 **Add a pointillize effect to a simple graphic image.** You can create an abstract, painterly quality by applying the pointillize effect. Select your image, choose Effect > Pixelate > Pointillize, enter a cell size, and click OK. The larger the cell size, the more abstract the effect. This example uses a cell size of 3.

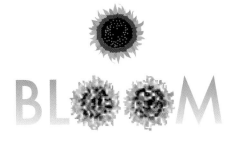

Here are examples of just a few of the graphic styles included in Illustrator CS. Use these preset effects to quickly add interesting surface texture to your artwork. Choose Window > Graphic Styles Libraries, and choose a library to display.

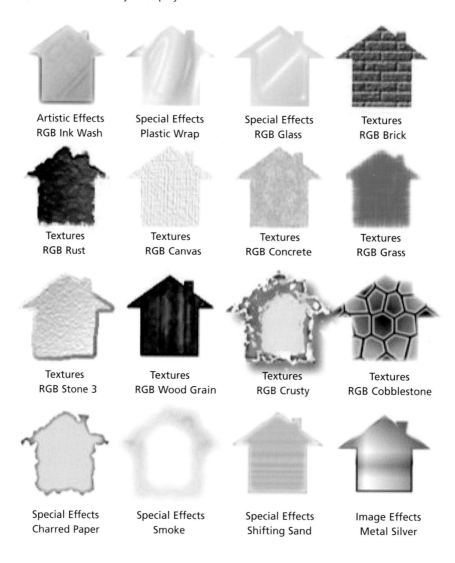

Artistic Effects	Special Effects	Special Effects	Textures
RGB Ink Wash	Plastic Wrap	RGB Glass	RGB Brick

Textures	Textures	Textures	Textures
RGB Rust	RGB Canvas	RGB Concrete	RGB Grass

Textures	Textures	Textures	Textures
RGB Stone 3	RGB Wood Grain	RGB Crusty	RGB Cobblestone

Special Effects	Special Effects	Special Effects	Image Effects
Charred Paper	Smoke	Shifting Sand	Metal Silver

To learn how these effects were created, simply apply the effect to a shape, and with the shape selected, choose Window > Appearance and then double-click the effect to view the specific settings.

Jazz Up Your Photos Without Leaving Illustrator

Transform photos using transparency blending mode overlays.

Dynamic photo effects in Illustrator? You bet. You can create some amazing effects using transparency blending modes. The effects will work in both RGB and CMYK color modes with differing results. You will start this project with an overlay that transforms a photo from color to a sepia tone.

1 **Get started.** Open a new CMYK color mode file. Choose File > Place. In the Place dialog box, navigate to any color photo file and click Place.

2 **Convert the image to black and white.** Select the image and choose Filter > Colors > Convert to Grayscale.

▷ **Note:** You need to convert color photos to black and white only when you want to apply sepia and other one-color tonal effects.

3 **Set the color for your overlay.** In the toolbox, make sure that the Fill box is in front by selecting its icon. In the Color palette, enter 20 for C, 34 for M, 29 for Y, 4 for K. This combination creates a warm sepia tone. Drag the Fill color from the toolbox to your Swatches palette to save it.

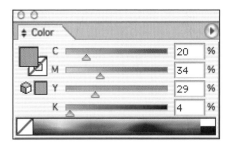

4 **Overlay your image.** Select the Rectangle tool in the toolbox. Click the swatch you saved in the Swatches palette. Drag the Rectangle tool marquee over your image to cover it.

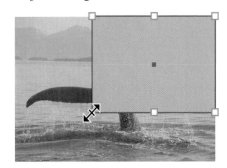

▷ **Note:** Smart Guides, found in the View menu, can help you get a precise fit over your photo image.

5 **Create the photo overlay.** Make sure that the sepia color covering your photo is selected. In the Transparency palette, choose the Multiply blending mode from the pop-up menu. Every photo image has different balances of light and dark. Experiment with the Transparency palette opacity percentages to get the best results for your image. For this image, 100% works best.

6 **Experiment with color.** Select your overlay and try different overlay colors and opacity settings to get some fun results. This technique is a good way to get the effect of a duotone photograph without leaving Illustrator.

Variation: Create striking color shifts from a color photo

1 **Open a color photo image in the RGB color mode.** Open a new RGB color mode file. Choose File > Place. In the Place dialog box, navigate to any color photo file and click Place.

2 **Create the first color in the overlay.** In the Color palette, enter 255 for R, 127 for G, and 0 for B. With the Fill color selected, use the Rectangle tool to drag an overlay to cover your image. In the Transparency palette, with the overlay selected, choose the Difference blending mode and 100% opacity.

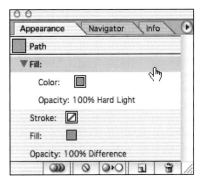

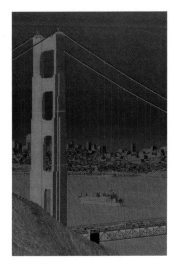

3 **Create the second color in the overlay.** If the Appearance palette is not
open, choose Window > Appearance.
Make sure that the overlay is selected.
Click the top right arrow button to
display the Options menu and choose
Add New Fill.

With the new Fill in the Appearance
palette still selected, in the Color
palette enter 102 for R, 187 for G,
80 for B to set your second color. In
the Transparency palette, choose the
Hard Light blending mode at 100%
opacity.

As you can see, using transparency
blending modes with color overlays
on images can produce some dramatic
results. Experiment in both RGB and
CMYK modes to see what you can
create.

Note: When adding more than one
color to your overlay, use the Appearance palette to get more consistent
effects.

The following examples were produced in CMYK color mode. Experiment in RGB color mode for some surprising results. You can save your results by selecting your overlay and dragging it into the Styles palette. Create a style library for your overlays; see the *Adobe Illustrator CS User Guide* for more information.

Overlay

Hue

Add more than one transparency blending mode overlay.

Saturation

Soft Light

Create a shape to add focus to your photo.

Overlay a pattern and experiment with blending modes.

Materials:

Postcard 3 template

Project 15

Manipulate Colors with Meshes

With the ability to flow colors in different directions, the Mesh tool gives the control you need to create realistic-looking illustrations.

By applying a fine mesh to an object and manipulating the color of mesh points and patches, you can achieve very realistic illustrations. In this project, against the background of the Post Card 3.ait template, you will create a ruby grapefruit as a mesh object and fine-tune it with the Mesh tool.

1 Get started. Choose File > New from Template. In the New from Template dialog box, choose Templates > Cards and Post Cards > Post Card 3.ait and click New from Template. Save and rename the file. In the Layers palette, lock all layers except Artwork by clicking their edit column buttons (next to the eye icons).

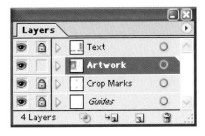

Select the orange gradient background, and lock it (Object > Lock > Selection). With the Group Selection tool, drag from just below the pear's stem down and just below the bottom green fringe, and delete the selections. Repeat as needed to select and delete all but the pear's stem.

2 Create a mesh object. To easily identify the swatches you will be using in this lesson, click the arrow button in

the Swatches palette to display the palette menu and choose List View.

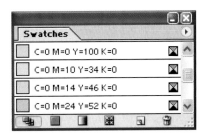

Select the Ellipse tool, and click the C=0 M=50 Y=100 K=0 swatch in the Swatches palette. Hold down Alt/ Option, and drag outward from the center of the background to create an oval roughly the shape of a grapefruit, about one half-inch from the postcard's edge. Choose Object > Create Gradient Mesh. In the dialog box, enter 4 for Rows, enter 4 for Columns, choose Flat for Appearance, and click OK. Deselect the artwork.

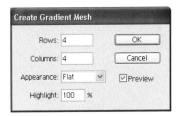

Mesh point

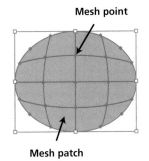

Mesh patch

3 **Add color to the object.** To help you in selecting mesh points, turn on Smart Guides (View > Smart Guides). Select the Direct Selection tool in the toolbox. Hold down Shift and click the center mesh point; then Shift-click the mesh point directly above it and the mesh point to its right. In the Swatches palette, select the C=0 M=24 Y=52 K=0 swatch.

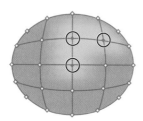

Next, click the Direct Selection tool on the left-edge mesh point directly below the center line; then Shift-click the rest of the mesh points on the grapefruit's bottom edge (as shown in the illustration). In the Swatches palette, select the C=0 M=63 M=100 K=30 swatch.

Click the mesh point directly below and to the right of center. In the Color palette, enter 60 for M, to redden the color. Drag the new color from the Fill button in the toolbox into the Swatches palette to save it. Select the Paint Bucket tool (grouped with the

Eyedropper tool) in the toolbox. Then click the tool on the next two mesh points to the left and on the mesh point directly above.

4 **Refine the art.** Select the Mesh tool and click it on the top edge from left to right between the vertical lines to add four more columns to the mesh object.

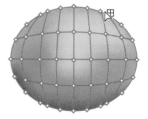

By adding mesh points, you automatically give the illustration more detail. You can refine the illustration even more by clicking mesh points with the Direct Selection tool and adjusting their color using the color sliders in the Color palette.

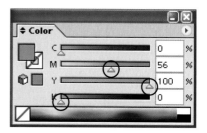

The objective is to get a smooth transition between the light and dark colors in the illustration.

5 **Add the stem and leaf.** With the Selection tool, select the stem in the artwork and drag it down to join the top of the grapefruit. In the Symbols palette, drag Leaf 1 onto the artwork. Double-click the Rotate tool and, in the Rotate dialog box, enter 60° for Angle.

Drag the leaf to connect near the base of the stem. To place the leaf behind the grapefruit and in front of the stem, press Ctrl/Command+X to copy it to the clipboard; then select the grapefruit, and press Ctrl/Command+B. Deselect.

6 **Add a drop shadow.** Select the grapefruit. Choose Effect > Stylize > Drop Shadow. In the Drop Shadow dialog box, select the Darkness option at the bottom of the palette and click OK. If you like, add design elements. Unlock the text layer and change the text to your liking. The text added here is Charlemagne Standard Bold, 24 point.

□ **Variation: Create a colorful design element in a few easy steps**

1 **Get started.** Open a new CMYK color mode file. Select the Ellipse tool. In the Swatches palette, click the Steel Cylinder swatch for the fill. Draw a circle on the artboard. In the Gradient palette, select the Radial option.

2 **Create a gradient mesh.** Choose
Object > Expand. In the Expand dialog box, select Gradient Mesh and
click OK.

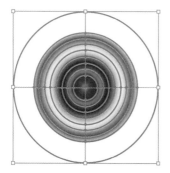

3 **Add color.** Drag solid color swatches
in the Swatches palette onto the
image's mesh points or mesh patches.
Color the design to your liking.

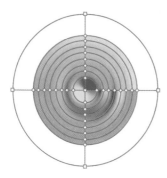

For the greatest control over your design when using the Gradient Mesh command or Mesh tool, start with a few mesh rows and columns.

To create a mesh object with the Mesh tool, draw a black-filled square on the artboard. Deselect the square and click another solid color in the Swatches palette. Select the Mesh tool and click three different points on top of the square's edge. Deselect, and click another solid color in the Swatches palette. Click a couple of times on the top edge, between the mesh lines you just created. Deselect the square and select another color in the Swatches palette. Click a couple of times on the bottom edge of the square with the Mesh tool. The more times you apply the Mesh tool, the more complex the mesh object becomes.

Starting with a simple mesh object gives you much more control over the design process. When you start out with too many mesh points and lines, you can waste a lot of time adjusting color and deleting mesh points to achieve the desired result.

Make Images Pop with 3D

Add another dimension to your art with Adobe Illustrator's newest feature, 3D.

With Illustrator 3D effects, it's now easy to make your designs jump right off the page. In this project, you will create a face icon and then apply 3D effects to it. You'll also have a chance to work with symbols from the 3D Symbols library.

1 **Get started.** Open a new CMYK color mode file. In the toolbox, click the Stroke button and then click None (☐). Click the Fill button to make it active. In the Swatches palette (Window > Swatches), click the Peach swatch. Select the Ellipse tool. Hold down Alt/Option+Shift and draw a circle on the artboard for the face. Deselect.

2 **Add the facial features.** In the Swatches palette, click the Black swatch. With the Ellipse tool, draw a small oval for an eye. In the toolbox, click the Selection tool. Alt/Option-drag to the right a short distance to duplicate the eye, pressing Shift as you drag to constrain the movement. Select both eye shapes and group them (Ctrl/Command+G). Select the Ellipse tool and draw a small circle for the nose and a larger oval for the

mouth. With the Selection tool, select the facial shapes and adjust their positions in the circle to resemble the following illustration. Then Shift-click all of the facial features and the face circle. In the Align palette (Shift+F7), click the Horizontal Align Center option.

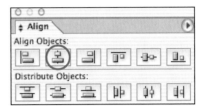

To subtract the facial shapes from the circle, choose Window > Pathfinder. In the Pathfinder palette, Alt/Option-click the Subtract from Shape Area button.

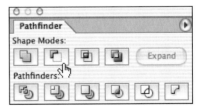

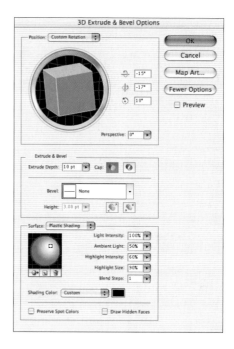

3 **Apply a 3D effect.** With the illustration selected, choose Effect > 3D Extrude & Bevel. In the 3D Extrude & Bevel dialog box, click Preview to see its default settings applied to your image.

4 **Adjust the 3D settings.** By changing the 3D settings in the dialog box, you can modify many of the image's 3D attributes. Apply your own settings in the dialog box, or apply the following settings to get the results as shown in the illustration at the end of this step. In the Position area, enter −15 for rotation around the X axis, enter −17 for rotation around the Y axis, and enter 10 for rotation around the Z axis. In Extrude & Bevel, enter 10 for Extrude Depth. Click More Options, and in Surface enter 1 for Blend Steps. Click OK.

5 **Expand and refine the art.** To change elements in the illustration, you need to expand it. Select the illustration and choose Object > Expand Appearance. Deselect the artwork. With the Group Selection tool, click the front of the face. In the Swatches palette, click the Midday Sky gradient swatch. Drag the Orange swatch over the right (dark blue) stop in the Gradient palette to change its color.

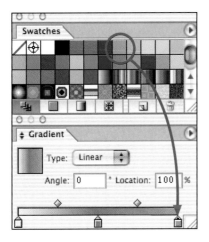

In the Color palette, enter 20 for K to darken the orange. In the Swatches palette, drag the Peach swatch over the middle (medium blue) stop in the Gradient palette to change its color. Next, drag the Custard swatch over the left (light blue) stop in the Gradient palette. In the toolbox, select the Gradient tool and drag it from the top of the face to the bottom.

Variation: Experiment with the 3D Symbols library

Get started. Open the 3D Symbols library (Window > Symbol Libraries > 3D Symbols). Drag any 3D symbol onto the artboard. To edit the symbol, click the Break Link to Symbol button at the bottom of the Symbols palette (press Shift+F11 if the palette is not open). Ungroup the selection (Ctrl/Command+Shift+G). In the Appearance palette, double-click Extrude and Bevel (under Fill) and experiment with the settings in the dialog box.

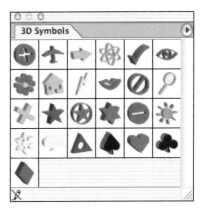

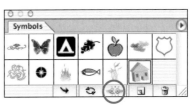

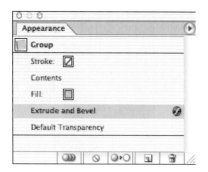

○ **Note:** In the Position area of the 3D Extrude and Bevel Options dialog box, drag the blue and gray box around its axis to quickly change the image's orientation. Make sure that Preview is checked to see the changes on the artboard.

☐ **Variation: Create a 3D text effect**

① **Get started.** Open a new CMYK color mode file. In the toolbox, select the Type tool. In the Character palette, select Myrid Pro Black (or another sans serif font) in the Font menu and enter 100 for the font size.

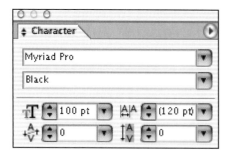

② **Create the text.** Type the word *Dynamic* in the artwork. In the toolbox, click the Selection tool. Choose Window > Swatches, and in the Swatches palette click the Lime swatch.

Dynamic

③ **Transform the text to 3D.** Choose Effects > 3D > Extrude & Bevel. In the Extrude & Bevel dialog box, click Preview. Change settings and experiment with the shading options until you achieve the desired result; then click OK. Choose Object > Envelope Distort > Make with Warp. In the Warp Options dialog box, click Preview and experiment with its settings. Click OK when you are satisfied.

Choose Object > Expand. In the Expand dialog box, click OK to apply the default settings. With the Group Selection tool, Shift-click the face of the text and experiment with color changes.

The 3D Revolve feature revolves open and closed paths around a central axis. Sometimes the results are unexpected. Try these two examples.

With the Ellipse tool, draw a stroked circle with no fill on the artboard. Double-click the Scale tool, and in the Scale dialog box, enter 60 for Scale, click Scale Strokes & Effects (if it is not already checked), and click Copy. Select both circles, and in the Pathfinder palette, click the Divide button. Choose Effect > 3D > Revolve, and click Preview to see the default settings applied to your image. In Revolve, enter 180 for Angle and click OK. To edit the illustration, select it and double-click 3D Revolve in the Appearance palette. In the 3D Revolve Options dialog box, experiment with the settings on the image.

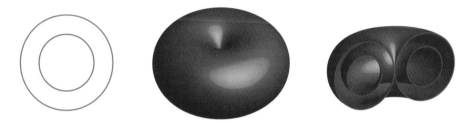

With the Pen tool, draw a stroke with no fill on the artboard. Copy the following image or draw an open path of your own. Choose Effect > 3D > Revolve. Click the Preview button to see the default settings applied to your image. Experiment with the dialog box option settings to see what happens.

Quickly Design a Web Page Template

The precision tools in Adobe Illustrator make quick work of designing great Web pages.

Designing a Web page is a breeze when you start with one of the pre-built Web page templates in Illustrator CS, located in the Templates folder. You can easily modify these templates using the collection of Web elements found in the Window menu under Symbol Libraries.

In this project, you will design a Web page template. You can then easily add your own content to complete the page design. The techniques used to create an active Web page will not be covered in this lesson.

1 **Get started.** Open a new file (Ctrl/Command+N). In the New Document dialog box, set Units to Pixels; then Enter 800 pixels for Width and 600 pixels for Height to create the dimensions of a standard Web page. For the Color Mode option, click RGB Color. Click OK.

Choose Window > Show Rulers. In the upper left corner box where the vertical and horizontal rulers meet, drag the pointer to reposition the ruler origin, so that the cross hairs line up with the left vertical and the top horizontal edges of the artboard.

2 **Create the template block.** In the toolbox, set the stroke to None. Click the Fill button and select Dried Sage in the Swatches palette. Select the Rectangle tool and Alt/Option-click in the center of the artboard. In the Rectangle dialog box, enter 800 pixels for Width and 600 pixels for Height and click OK. If the Transform palette is not open, choose Window > Transform. In the Transform palette, enter 400 pixels for X and –300 pixels for Y to center the rectangle on the artboard.

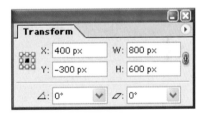

3 **Use guides and the Transform palette to structure the template.** Choose View > Guides and, in the drop-down menu, uncheck Lock Guides. Drag a guide from the top horizontal ruler into the top portion of the template. Make sure that the guide is still selected and, in the Transform palette, enter –70 for Y. Drag a guide from the left vertical ruler into the template. Make sure the guide is selected and, in the Transform palette, enter 170 pixels for X. Drag a second vertical guide into the template and, in the Transform palette, enter 720 pixels for X.

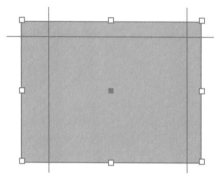

4 **Divide the template.** Select all elements (Select > All) and click the Divide button in the Pathfinder palette. Ungroup the image (Ctrl/Command+G) and deselect it (Ctrl/Command+Shift+A).

5 **Color the template.** Use the Swatches palette to color the template segments: select the top left template segment and click Black. Select the top middle segment and click Denim. Color the top right segment Orange, the left vertical segment Pine, and the right vertical segment Cuban Lime.

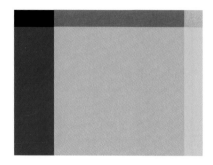

6 **Add the first main menu button.** Choose Window > Symbol Libraries > Web Buttons and Bars. In the Web Buttons and Bars Symbol library, click the arrow button and choose List View from the palette menu. For help in placing the buttons in the template, turn on Smart Guides (Ctrl/Command+U). With the Group Selection tool, drag an instance of Button 15 Mouse Down from the Web Buttons and Bars symbol library onto the template and place the button below the top left black rectangle. Zoom in on the area. Place the tool's pointer over the top left button's anchor point, and drag the anchor point to the black rectangle's lower left anchor point. The button will snap into place when the anchor points meet.

7 **Add additional buttons.** Next, drag an instance of Button 15 Mouse Normal from the Web Buttons and Bars symbol library onto the artboard and, place it below the first button. Zoom in on the area. Place the Group Selection tool's pointer on the button's top left anchor point and drag the top anchor point to the lower left anchor point of the first button until it snaps into place. Drag as many Button 15 Normal instances as you need for your template from the Web Buttons and Bars symbol library and snap them into place below each other.

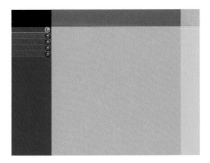

You now have a basic Web page template that can be configured for all of your Web pages. In this case, the menu's top button appearance indicates that the Web page is active. This button is not an active link.

Button 15 Mouse Down Symbol, active page

The remaining buttons indicate active page links. When processed into an HTML document, the top button art will be used as the rollover state for the active buttons. When configuring the template for each menu button, use the mouse-down instance to indicate it as the active page, and use the mouse-normal instance for the other menu buttons.

Button 15 Mouse Down Symbol, active page

8 **Add design elements and text.** Using the Type tool, name your buttons. Because a site normally opens to the home page, name the top button Home and color it differently than the active linked buttons. To show that the home page is the active page, you may want to italicize it. Choose Window > Symbol Libraries > Web Icons. Drag an instance of Home from the Web Icons library and place it in the upper left corner of the Dried Sage colored rectangle.

Scale the icon up 200%. Add a logo and other design elements to your liking. If you are not an expert illustrator, explore Illustrator's libraries and template folders for design elements to use for your Web pages.

Variation: Color-code your linked Web pages

Large Web sites that use the same template for each linked page can get a bit boring. Change the template's color for each main menu link to add some variety and to let the viewers know that they have arrived at a different location in your Web site.

1 **Get started.** Use the template you created for the project. Keep the top horizontal template segments the same color to maintain some continuity throughout the Web site.

2 **Change the colors.** Choose Window > Swatch Libraries and select any of the several swatch libraries to color the left, middle, and right template segments. Look at the color values in the original template and choose colors that harmonize with them.

Variation: Modify template menu buttons

1 **Get started.** Choose File > New from Template > Templates > Business Sets > BusSet 3 Web Site.ait and click New from Template.

Next, choose Window > Symbol Libraries > Web Buttons and Bars. Click the arrow button in the palette to display the palette menu options and select Small List View.

2 **Modify and color the new buttons.** Drag an instance of Button 28 Mouse Normal and Button 28 Mouse Down onto the artboard. Select them and break their links by clicking the Break Link to Symbol button in the Symbols palette. Deselect.

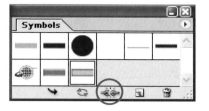

With the Group Selection tool, click

and delete the black vertical line at the left end of each button. Select the dark-gray center of Button 28 Mouse Normal and change its color by clicking the light-blue swatch in the Swatches palette. Shift-click the top and bottom light-gray areas of the button and color them with the dark blue.

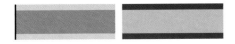

Next, click the light-gray center of Button 28 Mouse Down and color it dark blue; then Shift-click the dark-gray top and bottom areas of the button and color them light blue.

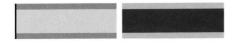

3 **Size the buttons.** Drag an instance of Main Menu Normal from the Symbols palette onto the artboard.

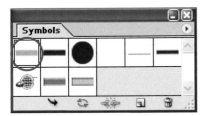

With the button selected, look in the Transform palette and note the button's height and width (68 pixels x 16 pixels). Delete the selection. Select the recolored Button 28 Mouse Normal and change its dimensions by entering 68 pixels for W and 16 pixels for H in the Transform palette. Next select the recolored Button 28 Mouse Down and change its dimensions in the Transform Palette to 68 pixels for W and 16 pixels for H.

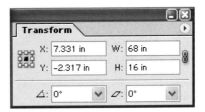

4 **Change the Web page's main menu buttons.** Select the altered Button 28 Mouse Normal and Alt/Option-drag it over the Main Menu Normal symbol in the Symbols palette to change its attributes; then delete the button from the artboard. Next, select the altered Button 28 Mouse Down and Alt/Option-drag it over the Main Menu Mouse Down symbol in the Symbols palette; delete the symbol from the artboard. Note the changes in the Web page's top menu buttons.

Open other Web templates and apply the above technique to modify their menu buttons.

Splash pages are a gateway to your Web site. Keep them simple and make the content reflect the nature of your site. You can configure a splash page to close shortly after loading or to remain in the browser window until a button is clicked. You can write a cookie to detect whether a viewer has visited the site; if the user has been to the site before, the browser will go directly to the home page.

Use the Web template you just created and delete everything except the background segments (or complete up to step 4 in the first part of the project). Select the Type tool and, in uppercase, type *WELCOME* in the center of the design; then click the Selection tool. In the Character palette, enter 80 pt for Font Size and select Arial Black Regular for Font. Choose Window > Graphic Style Libraries > 3D Effects. Select Emergence in the 3D Effects style library to apply the style to the text. Select the Type tool again and enter 24 pt for Font Size and choose Arial Bold for Font. In lowercase and just below *WELCOME*, type *enter at your own risk*. Open the Web Icons symbol library (Window > Symbol Libraries > Web Icons) and drag the symbol Forward onto your template. Position Forward to the right of the *enter at your own risk* text. The symbol and the text will be the active link to your home page.

Create a Web Banner Ad

Eye-catching banners are an effective way to advertise
your business or grab attention.

Good design and a short, focused message are the ingredients for an effective, attention-grabbing banner ad. In this project, you will create the elements for a full-size animated banner ad.

This project covers only the design of banner ads. Use Adobe ImageReady software or another Web tool application to convert the banner layers to an animated GIF or image rollover.

1 **Get started.** Open a new file (Ctrl/Command+N). In the New Document dialog box, choose Letter for Size, Pixels for Units, and RGB Color Mode; click OK.

2 **Create the first frame background.** In the Swatches palette, click the New Leaf swatch for the fill and, in the toolbox, set the stroke to None. Select the Rectangle tool and click the center of the artboard to open the Rectangle dialog box; enter 468 pixels for Width and 60 pixels for Height and click OK. This rectangle will be the background.

3 **Add the ladybug.** Choose Window > Symbol Libraries > Web Buttons and Bars. Drag Button 37 Normal (the orange ladybug) and place it at the far right of the background. Rotate the ladybug button counterclockwise

by double-clicking the Rotate tool to open the Rotate dialog box and entering 90° for Angle.

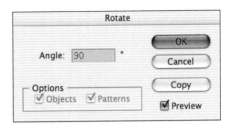

4 **Add the text.** Select the Type tool and click at the far left edge of the background. In the Swatches palette, select the Cuban Lime swatch for the fill. In the Type palette, select Myriad Pro Bold Italic (or another sans serif italic) for Font and set the font size to 36 point. Type *Bugged about aphids?*

Bugged about aphids?

5 **Apply 3D to the text.** Click the Selection tool and choose Effect > 3D > Extrude & Bevel to open the Extrude & Bevel Options dialog box. In the Position section, enter –18° for the X axis (top option), 10° for the Y axis (middle option), and 0° for the Z axis (bottom option). In the Extrude & Bevel section of the dialog box, enter 10 pt for Extrude Depth. Click the More Options button and, in the Surface section, drag the light to the center of the sphere. Click OK.

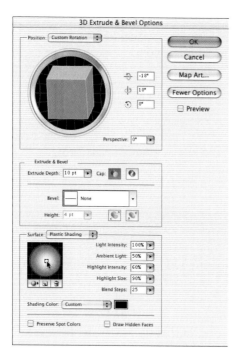

7 **Create the second animation frame.** In the Layers palette, drag Layer 1 to the New Layer button at the bottom of the palette. Double-click Layer 1 Copy (the top layer) in the palette and, in the Layer Options dialog box, name the layer Frame One; then double-click Layer 1 (the bottom layer) and name it Frame Two. Toggle off the eye icon in the Frame One layer to make the layer invisible.

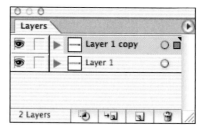

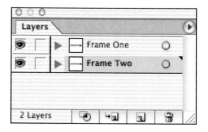

6 **Add a drop shadow.** Choose Effect > Stylize > Drop Shadow. In the Drop Shadow dialog box, enter 2.16 pixels for X Offset, 2.16 pixels for Y Offset, and 2.16 pixels for Blur, and click OK. Select all of the design elements (Ctrl/Command+A) and, in the Align palette, click the Vertical Align Center button.

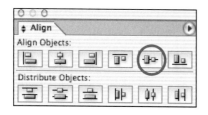

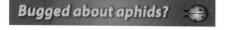

8 **Edit the second frame.** Select the Type tool, triple-click the text in the Frame Two layer, and change it to *Click here for relief!* Click the Selection tool in the toolbox to select the text. In the Swatches palette, click the Yellow swatch. Deselect the text and select the ladybug. Double-click the Rotate tool and, in the Rotate dialog box, enter 180° and click OK. Select the background and, in the Swatches palette, change the fill to Orange.

9 **Finish the frame.** Choose Window > Symbol Libraries > Arrows and drag Arrow 4 between the text and the ladybug. In the Symbols palette, click the Break Link to Symbol button. Select the Eyedropper tool and click the text to add its attributes to the arrow. Change the arrow's color to white in the Swatches palette to complete the banner ad's second animation frame.

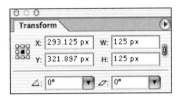

Toggle the Frame One layer eye icon on and off to preview the animation.

Banner ads are designed in standard sizes. You can find banner ad sizes and other important Web standards information at Interactive Advertising Bureau's site (www.iab.net).

Variation: Make a smaller Web banner

Often, you will want to create several versions of the same banner using different Web standard dimensions.

1 **Get started.** Use the banner ad you created for the project. Make sure that both frames are visible. With the Selection tool, drag into the banner's background to select both frame backgrounds. In the Transform palette, enter 125 pixels for W and 125 pixels for H; press Tab to

set the new dimensions. (If the chain icon does not look like the icon in the following example, click it to independently change your selection's Width and Height dimensions.)

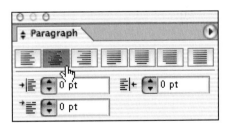

2 **Adjust the text.** You'll add carriage returns and reduce the type size. In the toolbox, select the Type tool and click its insertion point at the leading edge of the word *about* and press Enter/Return. Click the tool at the leading edge of the word *aphids* and press Enter/Return. Click the Selection tool. In the Character palette, set the font size to 22 points and in the Paragraph palette, select Align Center.

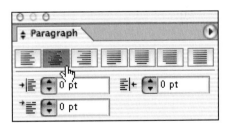

Toggle off the eye icon in the Frame One layer to make the layer's contents invisible. Select Frame Two in the Layers palette. With the Type tool, click the insertion point at the leading edge of the word *for* and press Enter/Return; then click the Selection tool. In the Character palette, set the font size to 22 points and click Align Center in the Paragraph palette. In the Layers palette, toggle on the Frame One layer to make its contents visible. Select the text of both layers and drag the text to the top center of the background square as shown in the following illustration.

Bugged
about
aphids?

Note: Don't forget that the banner contents are on two layers. You won't see the bottom layer's text when it is placed in position unless you toggle off the eye icon.

3 **Finish the banner.** Select both of the ladybugs on the artboard. Double-click the Scale tool to open the Scale dialog box and enter 70% for Uniform; then select Scale Strokes & Effects and click OK. Click the Selection tool and drag the ladybugs to the lower right corner of the banner. In the Layers palette, toggle off the Frame One layer eye icon to make the layer's contents invisible. Select the white arrow and drag it to the left of the ladybug. You now have two layer frames that can be used for an animated banner or rollover.

Toggle the Frame One layer eye icon on and off to preview the animation.

Frame 1   Frame 2

Illustrator's many image libraries offer a wealth of content that you can use to quickly design effective and professional banner ads.

Open a new RGB color mode file. Choose Windows > Symbols Libraries > Web Buttons and Bars. Drag Button 23 Normal onto the artboard. In the Layers palette, click the Create New Layer button; then drag Button 23 Mouse Down over the top of the first button. In the Layers palette, drag Layer 2 down under Layer 1. Select both buttons on the artboard and, in the Align palette, click Horizontal Align Center and Vertical Align Center. In the Transform palette, enter 125 pixels for Width and 125 pixels for Height and press Tab to set the new size. Deselect the buttons. Click Springfield Green in the Swatches palette; then select the top button. Choose the Symbol Strainer tool in the toolbox and click the top button to stain the button green. Next, toggle off the Layer 1 eye icon to make the layer's contents invisible. Select Layer 2. Click Magenta in the Swatches palette; then select the bottom button and click the Symbol Strainer tool on the button to stain it magenta. Add your content to the banner buttons; look in the image libraries for inspiration.

You now have a two-frame banner that can be made into an animated GIF or a rollover.

Frame 1

Frame 2

Index